DATE DUE

SE 14 '98			
AP 12 '00			
AP 21 '03			
JA 26 '06			
SE 23 '08			
SE 16 '08			

DEMCO 38-296

CORPORATE CRIME INVESTIGATION

Jack Bologna
and
Paul Shaw

Butterworth-Heinemann
Boston   Oxford   Johannesburg   Melbourne   New Delhi   Singapore

Library of Congress Cataloging-in-Publication Data
Bologna, Jack.
  Corporate crime investigation / by Jack Bologna and Paul Shaw.
      p.   cm.
  Includes bibliographical references (p.   ) and index.
  ISBN 0-7506-9659-1 (alk. paper)
  1. Commercial crimes—United States.   2. Employee theft—
  Investigation—United States.   3. Employee crimes—United States.
  4. Corporations—Corrupt practices—United States.   5. Industries—
  Security measures—United States.   6. Employees—Crimes against—
  United States.   7. White collar crime investigation—United States.
  I. Shaw, Paul, 1939– . II. Title.
  HF5549.5.E43B65   1996
  363.2'5968--dc20   96-42951
                                                                    CIP

British Library Cataloguing-in-Publication Data
A catalogue record for this book is available from the British Library.

The publisher offers special discounts on bulk orders of this book.
For information, please contact:

Manager of Special Sales
Butterworth-Heinemann
313 Washington Street
Newton, MA 02158-1626
Tel: 617-928-2500
Fax: 617-928-2620

For information on all Security publications available, contact our World Wide
Web home page at: http://www.bh.com

10 9 8 7 6 5 4 3 2 1

Printed in the United States of America

Contents

Preface

From the common law perspective, corporations could not commit crimes, mainly because corporations were "soul-less beings," and could not serve time if convicted of a crime. Over the years, through legislative action and U.S. Supreme Court opinions, corporations were made liable for their officers' criminal acts and became subject to fines but not imprisonment. Most recently, however, corporations, by way of their officers, can even serve time for crimes committed on their behalf by their officers and corporate agents. Today, corporate crime can be viewed from several perspectives:

- Crimes committed against corporations by officers, directors, and employees (fraud, theft, embezzlement, corruption)
- Crimes committed against corporations by external forces (robbery, burglary, larceny, piracy)
- Crimes—regulatory noncompliance, tax evasion, bribery, false financial statements—committed for corporations by internal forces (officers, directors, and senior employees)

Corporate crimes create a measure of embarrassment to officers, as well as the possibility of heavy fines and imprisonment. Corporate officers, therefore, have been reluctant to prosecute or even investigate their colleagues. Today, that policy may bring on some very rough treatment (e.g., heavy fines, long imprisonment) by the courts under the recently issued U.S. Sentencing Commission guidelines. As a result, it behooves corporate officers and their security, internal audit, and risk-management staffs to become more conversant with the guidelines themselves, with criminal laws, in general, and, thereafter, to take appropriate action—adopt codes of ethics, strengthen controls, take vigorous action when internal crimes are alleged and/or proven.

Accordingly, this book is intended to serve the needs of professional white-collar crime detectives, corporate security investigators, risk managers, and internal auditors, and also to serve the information needs of corporate officers, directors, and business writers. *Corporate Crime Investigation*, however, is not intended to serve as a legal reference for preparing cases but should be useful as a guide when corporations need to prevent, detect, and/or investigate suspected crimes against themselves.

A Primer on Corporate Fraud Detection

CORPORATE FRAUD DETECTION IN A NUTSHELL

In the corporate context, fraud can be categorized as internal—committed by insiders (e.g., officers, directors, employees, and agents)—and external—committed by outsiders (e.g., vendors, contractors, and suppliers). Corporate fraud also can be classified as to crimes committed by insiders against the company (e.g., theft, corruption, and embezzlement) and crimes committed by insiders for the company (e.g., violation of government regulations—tax, securities, safety, and environmental laws).

In a causative context, fraud is both personal and environmental. For example, fraud perpetrators generally are motivated by economic need or greed. Environmental factors that breed internal

Acknowledgment: Portions of this chapter have been excerpted with permission from the *Forensic Accounting Review*, 1994–1995.

fraud and create opportunities for embezzlement and theft include lax accounting controls and loose moral standards among the members of senior management. Often, corporate frauds are detected by accounting discrepancies noted by internal auditors and by allegations of theft, corruption, or embezzlement received by security investigators.

Frauds perpetrated by senior management involve the misrepresentation of facts in financial statements. In such cases, there may be overstatements of assets, sales and profits, or understatements of liabilities, expenses, and losses. Senior managers perpetrate financial statement frauds to deceive investors and lenders or to inflate profits and thereby gain higher salaries and bonuses.

Frauds committed by low-level employees include techniques such as falsifying expense reports and benefit claims; embezzling funds; using corporate property for personal purposes; stealing corporate property; and accepting gratuities from vendors, contractors, and suppliers. Low-level frauds are often called transaction frauds, as distinguished from fraud in financial statements mentioned previously. Transaction frauds are most likely to occur in environments in which motives, opportunities, means, and methods abound. The following conditions are indicative of a high level of risk for transaction frauds:

- Internal controls are absent, weak, or loosely enforced.
- Employees are hired without due consideration for their honesty and integrity.
- Employees are poorly managed, exploited, abused, or placed under great stress to accomplish financial goals and objectives.
- Management models are themselves corrupt, inefficient, or incompetent.
- A trusted employee has an insoluble personal problem, usually of a financial nature, brought about either by family medical needs, alcoholism, drug abuse, excessive gambling, or expensive tastes.
- The industry of which the company is a part has a history or tradition of corruption.
- The company has fallen on bad times (i.e., is losing money or marketshare), or its products or services are becoming passé.
- Internal audit resources are inadequate.
- Security resources are inadequate.

HOW TO DISCERN AND DETECT CORPORATE FRAUD

There is no simple cookbook recipe for conducting a fraud audit nor are there any generally accepted checklists or patterned interviews. Fraud is a human phenomenon. In terms of the techniques used to detect it, humans vary a great deal as do frauds. But, the following accounting "red flags" do give off some inkling of fraud:

- Adjusting journal entries that lack authorization and supporting details.
- Expenditures that lack supporting documents.
- False and improper entries in accounting books and records.
- Unauthorized payments.
- Unauthorized use of corporate assets.
- Misapplications of corporate funds.
- Destruction, counterfeiting, and forgery of documents that support payments.

In the process of committing such frauds, certain account balances may be overstated or understated; if the amount is small, detection will be difficult. The detection method is based on variance or exception notions of accounting.

Expectations of normal ranges are established for each account balance, and when variances are beyond the bounds of the expected high and low range, the account balance is flagged for further review and analysis. For example, review the cost of sales and gross profit, and what do you find? The probability that any business's gross profit would more than double (20% to 41%) in three years when sales rose much more modestly is highly remote unless the nature of its products and their markups changed dramatically or competition has changed dramatically (fewer competitors).

Although the relationship between sales and cost of sales is not a fixed or constant relationship, wide variances should cause an auditor to wonder what underlies such a gap. Some auditors call the signs used to monitor such gaps "red flags"; they do not prove fraud, but the "flags" do indicate that something in the cost of sales is out of whack. The gap may suggest that sales are overstated, returns and allowances are understated, or the account components of cost of sales are misstated (e.g., purchases and freight-in are understated). At any rate, it is time for the auditor to probe more deeply. Here are a few other red flags to look for:

- Is profit the only corporate objective and the only criteria for performance appraisal?
- Is the corporate culture one in which profit and economic incentives are the only motivators?
- Is there an effective code of corporate conduct?
- Are controls monitored for compliance?
- Are complaints from customers, stockholders, employees, and vendors ignored?
- Are management overrides of internal controls monitored?

Table 1–1 shows how a fraud can evolve.

Table 1–1   Evolution of an Accounting System Fraud

1. Motivation
   - Need, greed, revenge
2. Opportunity
   - Access to assets and records
3. Control weaknesses
   - No audit trails or separation and rotation of duties
   - No internal audit function, no control policies, no ethics code
4. Formulation of intent
   - Rationalization of crime as borrowing, not stealing
5. Act of theft, fraud, or embezzlement
6. Concealment
   - Alteration, forgery, or destruction of records
7. Red flags
   - Variances detected, allegations made, behavior pattern change noted
8. Audit initiated
   - Discrepancies detected
9. Investigation initiated
   - Evidence gathered, loss of assets confirmed and documented, interrogation of principals
10. Prosecution recommended
    - Civil recovery sought, insurance claim filed
11. Trial
    - Presentation of facts and testimony

When an allegation of employee fraud, theft, embezzlement, or corruption is received by a corporate security investigator, procedures to verify fraud should include: (1) assessing the credibility of the complainant and the plausibility of his or her charges; (2) determining whether testimonial, documentary, and demonstrative evidence is available to support the allegation; and (3) preparing a report of the facts, as determined thus far, and submitting same to in-house counsel for permission to open an active case.

2

Lying, Cheating, and Stealing—Is It Still the Same?

The following interview was conducted with a gentleman who was an accountant in New York City for more than forty years. Because of his former positions and assignments, he wishes to remain anonymous. He has been involved in fraud cases and has dealt with a variety of companies and organizations in his career. Because he has seen fraud close up for such a span of time, we feel his insights are worth sharing with you.

QUESTION: It has been said that only about ten basic schemes account for ninety percent of company frauds. Do you believe this to be true?

ANSWER: I don't know whether there are ten basic schemes or a hundred, but as many basic schemes as there are, the variations are compounded immeasurably according to the variety of intelligence, greed, and opportunities available to the perpetrators.

QUESTION: What do you think company policy and procedure should be for reporting fraudulent acts?

ANSWER: A suspicious or confirmed discovery should be reported immediately to the proper official of the company or organization. The proper official may be the chief internal auditor, controller, or legal counsel; in a smaller firm, it could be the president.

If the reporting is done immediately, the correct procedure can be pursued by management to protect itself and to recover whatever assets were lost. And, reporting immediately allows that official to determine whether legal counsel is required, as for instance, if the fraud was of such a nature that it might trigger a liability or negligence suit against the corporation or management. Legal counsel can determine whether the discovered incident should be reported to public authorities, such as the local district attorney, the SEC, or another authority that might have jurisdiction.

QUESTION: Who should conduct the initial investigation of a possible fraud?

ANSWER: Who should investigate depends on the kind of incident that was discovered. If the incident can be seen as affecting the maintenance of the books, then it should be the accountant or auditor. The incident may be purely a bookkeeping problem, where, in order to obtain a trial balance, certain accounts were manipulated to balance the books. Or, when an act discovered in one department might affect another department; for example, the theft of merchandise might be covered up by fictitious bookkeeping entries or by shifting payments to indicate that the merchandise stolen was paid for.

The security department should investigate any theft or unauthorized use of physical property. Sometimes, of course, accountants, security personnel, and legal counsel may be required. And, you may need to get outside assistance in the form of CPAs, lawyers, investigators, plus forensic experts, to establish evidence for prosecution or recovery.

QUESTION: In an investigation of company fraud, to what extent should an accountant/investigator seek legal counsel regarding evidence, privileged communication, and interviewing suspects?

ANSWER: The accountant should seek legal advice regarding the extent to which he or she should investigate to obtain evidence based on what seems to be the complexity of the incident. The accountant should discuss with legal counsel to what extent and which accounting records, underlying data, and original documents should be protected and preserved and by what means.

Any information must be revealed as long as the accountant is not involved in the incident. If he or she is involved, the accountant has the privilege against self-incrimination. If the accountant is an employee of the corporation, any information that is between the attorney and himself or herself is privileged. This is because the corporation that employs the accountant is the principal involved and it has privileged communication with the attorney.

When interviewing suspects in a fraud case, the accountant should definitely consult with the attorney as to legal limitations and possible liabilities. An independent outside auditor or CPA should not be obligated under his or her retainer to obtain any confession, oral or written; that person's duty and obligation is only to find evidence in the books of account and underlying records.

QUESTION: How deeply can an investigator, with a knowledge of basic accounting, investigate an average fraud or embezzlement?

ANSWER: An investigator with only a knowledge of basic accounting should not think that she or he can investigate even the average fraud or embezzlement. Investigation requires a knowledge of the business, of the type of fraud and its variations, of the organization's internal controls, as well as the possible avenues the fraud might lead to before anyone can even think of how detailed an investigation should be made. Often, what appears to be an average fraud or embezzlement may turn out to be either a mistake or a simple error; or the opposite extreme where a Pandora's box is opened affecting top management and outsiders.

If the investigator has sufficient expertise and experience, it may be possible to quickly determine how deeply he or she may have to go, although it probably would be best to consult legal and accounting talent to determine to what extent an investigation is necessary.

QUESTION: Should a CPA be brought in to investigate most or all financial crimes?

ANSWER: It would be advisable to bring in an accountant. First, as a possible expert witness; second, to determine to what extent the company's financial position is affected by the crime. In addition, certain contracts, such as insurance, bonding, and protection policies, may require a CPA audit of the books.

QUESTION: Can an accountant advise management or corporate security on ways to prevent or detect fraud?

ANSWER: An accountant can be very useful in devising a system of internal controls that would warn of opportunities for fraud, embezzlement, or other financial crimes. An accountant can also be useful in advising on a division of labor so that the internal control system can be implemented, and any crimes or unauthorized diversions that do occur can be discovered quickly and investigations pursued along proper channels.

QUESTION: Do you believe fraudulent acts are becoming more complex and more difficult to investigate?

ANSWER: I don't believe that fraudulent acts are becoming more complex. An embezzlement is an embezzlement no matter how it's performed. Complexity arises from the various types of businesses, the method of recording accounting transactions, the transactions themselves, and the degree of reliance on the computer. If an analysis of transactions is required, it becomes complex to ascertain the facts that occurred.

QUESTION: Does it seem that embezzlers and other white-collar criminals are getting smarter?

ANSWER: I cannot assume that embezzlers and criminals are getting smarter. Years ago it was said that most white-collar crime was committed by trusted employees. And crimes occurred when there was a lack of awareness and controls and an overdose of greed. I believe that still holds. There may be different variations of the crimes to get around computer technology but fundamentally, the causes of crime are the same.

QUESTION: What do you think are basic contributing factors to internal theft?

ANSWER: As long as there are people who want something for nothing, you'll have crime. And as long as reasonable alertness is not practiced by management and laxity of rules is allowed, the opportunities for fraud become more available. Two vital factors in internal theft are laxity and poor implementation of a company's internal controls. Also, when the bosses steal, you're bound to find instances of fraud and other crimes by employees because employees will imitate their bosses. Another thing often occurs too—the responsibility and liability of employees is hard to pinpoint.

3

A Taxonomy on Fraud

This treatise is on fraud in many of its forms and manifestations—
that is, consumer fraud, charity fraud, commercial fraud, computer
(and the Internet) fraud, telemarketing fraud, home-repair fraud,
investment fraud, medical fraud, personal improvement fraud, procurement fraud, business opportunity fraud, and embezzlement.
But, what do these individualized frauds have in common? *Fraud*,
by laymen's definition, is an intentional deception of another whose
property the perpetrator hopes to take by stealth or guile. In that
sense, fraud is lying, cheating, and stealing.

The same act of fraud can be a crime, a tort (civil wrong), and
a breach of contract. A fraudster can, therefore, be prosecuted, sued
civilly for damages, and sued for rescission of contract for the same
act of fraud. The crime of fraud and deceit is the most insidious of
all white-collar crimes in terms of number of incidents, dollars lost,
and psychological harm suffered by innocent victims.

Some frauds are business-related, others are nonbusiness-related.
Business-related frauds consist of dishonest practices by parties—
buyer/seller, lessor/lessee, employer/employee, principal/agent,
stockholder/corporation, banker/borrower, client/lawyer, and so
on—on either side of a business transaction. The frauds covered in

11

this taxonomy consist mainly of business-related frauds. (See Table 3–1).

Table 3–2 shows a top ten list for twelve kinds of fraud. The following is a list of the most common high-tech frauds:

1. Telephone toll fraud
2. Hardware/software theft
3. Software piracy
4. Proprietary information theft
5. Credit card counterfeiting
6. Wire tapping and bugging
7. Signal snagging
8. Password cracking
9. RFE reading
10. Hacking/phone phreaking
11. EFT fraud
12. e-mail reading
13. Credit card theft
14. Browsing/schmoozing

Table 3–1   A Taxonomy on Frauds

Against Stakeholders

Communities	Regulatory agencies
Creditors	Shareholders
Customers	Suppliers
Employees	

By Outsiders	*By Insiders*
Competitors	Abuse of assets
Contractors	Corruption
Customers	Embezzlement
Suppliers	Expense padding
Vendors	Performance fabrication
	Theft

Corporate Fraud Distinctions

1. Blue-collar/White-collar
2. Civil/Criminal/Contractual
3. Culture/Structure
4. Fraud auditing/Financial auditing
5. Fraud auditing/Forensic accounting
6. Fraud/Theft/Embezzlement
7. For/Against corporation
8. High-level/Low-level management
9. Honesty/Integrity
10. Internal/External fraudsters
11. Management/Nonmanagement
12. Motivations/Opportunities
13. Prevention/Detection
14. Profit/Nonprofit
15. Statement/Transaction

Victims of Fraud	*Perpetrators of Fraud*	
Organizations	Business owners	Hackers
Individuals	Corporate officers	Impersonators
Customers	Employees	Phone scams
Stockholders	Suppliers	Embezzlers
Creditors	Vendors	
Consumers	Competitors	
Bankers	Contractors	
Insurers	Consumers	
Investors	Customers	
Suppliers	Con artists	
Competitors	Inside traders	
Contractors	Counterfeiters	
	Forgers	

Fraudulent Schemes

Adulterated food	False advertising	**Medical**
Adulterated drugs	False representations	Overbilling
Arson	**False financial**	Password cracking
Bankruptcy	**statements**	**Personal**
Bid rigging	False entries	**improvement**
Breach of trust	False counts and	Pigeon drop
Business	weights	Price fixing
opportunities*	False packaging and	Prize winner
Charities	labeling	**Procurement**
Check kiting	False expense reports	Proprietary infor-
Commercial	False documentation	mation theft
Computer	**Financial statement**	Pyramid (*ponzi*)
Consumer	**frauds**	RFE (radio frequency
Corporation	Forgery	emanations) reading
(Chapter 9)	Hacking	Scams
Corruption	**Hi-tech**	Signal snagging
Counterfeiting	**Home repairs**	(interception of
Credit card theft	Impersonation	satellite and other
Electronic funds	Insider trading	transmissions)
transfer (EFT)	Insurance	Software piracy
e-mail	**Internet fraud** (see	Spanish prisoner
Embezzlement	page 16)	Substitution
(Chapter 8)	**Investment**	Sunken treasure
Fake jewelry	Lapping	**Telemarketing**
False accident, loss,	Larceny	Wire transfer
and damage claims	Mail	

---

*Items in bold are more fully developed later in this book.

Table 3–2   Top Ten List for Twelve Kinds of Fraud

Computer

1. Input frauds (entry of false data; data diddling)
2. Thruput frauds (programming fraud; salami slicing, trap doors, trojan horses, time bombs, logic bombs, etc.)
3. Output frauds (suppression of exceptions reports; theft of information)
4. Unauthorized access (hacking)
5. Scavenging (dumpster diving)
6. Shoulder surfing (stealing passwords)
7. Spoofing (false personation)
8. Imposter terminal
9. Social engineering (conning service personnel)
10. Pizza boy ploy

Financial Statement

1. Inventory overstatement
2. Early booking of sales
3. Expense deferral
4. Overstated assets
5. Understated liabilities
6. Overstated revenue
7. Understated expenses
8. Unrecorded expenses and liabilities
9. Lapping cash and receivables
10. False year-end adjustments

Embezzlement

1. Economic need or greed
2. Rationalization
3. Egocentric
4. Psychotic
5. Easy access to cash
6. Easy access to records
7. Inadequate supervision
8. Lapping and skimming
9. Concealment
10. False entries and false documentation

Home Repair

1. Furnace cleaning
2. Chimney rebuilding
3. Roof repairs
4. Replacement windows
5. Carpet cleaning
6. Exterior painting
7. Interior painting
8. Kitchen cabinet replacement
9. Plumbing repairs
10. Heating and air conditioning service

Charity

1. Police and firefighters
2. Widows and orphans charities
3. Poor and needy fundraising
4. Victims of disease
5. Victims of persecution
6. Victims of disasters
7. Handicapped children
8. Church fundraising for improvements
9. Research on terminal diseases
10. Victims of abuse

Medical

1. Unnecessary surgeries
2. Unnecessary diagnostic tests
3. Unnecessary treatments
4. Billing for fictitious services
5. Double billing
6. Faked industrial accidents
7. Faked auto accidents
8. Kickbacks
9. Referral fees
10. False claims for reimbursement

Business Opportunity

1. Worm farms
2. Franchise offerings
3. Vending machines
4. Antiques
5. Collectibles
6. Oriental rugs
7. Mail order sales
8. Sunken treasure
9. Lost gold mines
10. Water conditioners or household cleaning products

Procurement

1. Padding expenses
2. Inflating costs
3. Bid rigging
4. Low-balling bids
5. Price fixing
6. Corruption of bid reviewers
7. Double billing
8. Billing for unrelated expenses
9. Substitution of inferior parts, material, and workmanship
10. Short weights and counts

Commercial

1. Bankruptcy
2. Arson
3. Bank transactions
4. False medical claims
5. False damage and injury claims
6. False accident claims
7. False loss claims
8. False claims for refunds
9. False expense claims
10. False financial statements

Telemarketing

1. Prize winner scam
2. Unneeded insurance
3. High-risk investments
4. Florida real estate
5. Discount jewelry
6. Discount telephone services
7. Home modernization
8. Books and records
9. Fake charities
10. Free travel

Investment

1. Life insurance
2. Worthless stock
3. Insider trading
4. Penny stocks
5. Gold mines
6. Oil wells
7. Minerals
8. Real estate development
9. Franchise offerings
10. Pyramid schemes

Personal Improvement

1. Body-building spas
2. Weight-loss clinics
3. Dietary supplements
4. Vitamins, herbs, and home remedies
5. Hair and skin care products
6. Exercise equipment
7. Computer dating
8. Diploma mills
9. Dance studios
10. Speed reading

Consumer

1. False weights
2. False measures
3. False advertising
4. False packaging and labeling
5. False representations
6. Forgery
7. Counterfeiting
8. Impersonation
9. Adulterated food
10. Adulterated drugs

The following are some scams, tricks, and con games to be on the lookout for:

1. Fixed races
2. Stacked decks
3. Three-card monte
4. Marked cards
5. Fast shuffle
6. Loaded dice
7. Pigeon drop
8. Fortune telling

9. Seances
10. Shell game
11. Sleight of hand
12. Spanish prisoner
13. Fake documents of title
14. Counterfeit securities
15. Fake jewelry

But all is not lost. Fraud can be avoided if you remember the following bits of advice.

Avoiding Fraud

1. Study offers carefully. If they sound too good to be true, they probably are.
2. Be wary when time given to review an offer is minimal.
3. Be wary when appeals are made to your vanity, your ego, your greed, or your faith in God, country, and family.
4. Check out offer and offeror with the Better Business Bureau, state Attorney General, Federal Trade Commission, Securities and Exchange Commission, Dunn and Bradstreet and/or a credit service like TRW.
5. Check out offer and offeror with your lawyer, CPA, and banker.
6. Pay no money until equivalent value is delivered.
7. Weigh the risk and expected reward. If the promised reward exceeds current market rates for interest by two or more times, forget about the deal. It's probably a scam.

INTERNET FRAUD: THE NEW SCOURGE

The Internet is the largest unregulated information utility in the world today. Some 33 million users have direct access to it. Twice as many have indirect access. Most Internet users seek information sources—databases, bulletin boards, knowledgeable people, newspapers, magazines, books, and so on. Their main purpose in using the Internet is research and problem solving. But the Internet now offers far more than research services.

The Internet provides access to thousands of vendors of industrial and consumer products and services, including items such as stocks, bonds, mutual funds, money market accounts, business opportunities, jewelry, real estate, software, hardware, health spas, personal improvement courses, antiques, collectibles, franchises, legal and accounting services, travel services, computer dating, dance studios, diploma mills, exercise equipment, body-building spas, hair and skin care, weight loss, home remedies, and so on.

While the U.S. Congress frets and stews about pornography on the Internet, it does nothing about the billions of dollars consumers will pay for useless or worthless products and services. Indeed, the Congress of the late 1990s seems hell-bent on disbanding the very agencies that have provided some measure of protection to consumers (e.g., SEC, FTC, FDA).

$$4$$

Checklist of Fraud Indicators

The following are symptomatic of all frauds; there almost always is (1) an act or actors, (2) motivation for commission, (3) a means for commission, (4) an opportunity to commit the act, (5) an opportunity to profit from the act, and (6) the feeling "I won't get caught." Some of the most common frauds are:

- Invoicing for goods below set prices and then obtaining cash kickbacks from the purchasers.
- Increasing the amounts of suppliers' invoices and keeping the excess or splitting it with the suppliers.
- Paying suppliers' invoices twice (using the "Second Notice" invoice but keeping the second check). (Because this scheme depends on delaying payments until second invoices are received, the firm's credit rating can also be hurt.)
- Destroying delivery records or other evidence that some service was performed so that commission agents or others who collect from customers can pocket the proceeds, part of which goes to the employee who destroyed the records. (This is one of the rarer crimes.)
- Pocketing checks collected from presumably uncollectible accounts.

- Forging checks and destroying them when returned with bank statements. (The false transactions are concealed by forcing footings in cash books or by raising the amounts of legitimately returned checks.)
- Not charging "accommodation" purchases to employees or customers or hiding them in expense accounts.
- Failing to record returned purchases, allowances, and discounts, and keeping the difference.
- Padding payrolls as to rates, times, or amounts produced. (Adding false names, "ghosts," to the payroll is now a largely extinct fraud because of the need to make deductions and create W-2 forms.)
- Issuing checks in payment of invoices from fictitious suppliers and cashing them through the dummy company.
- Pocketing the proceeds of cash sales and not recording the transactions.
- "Lapping"—pocketing small amounts from incoming payments and then applying subsequent remittances on other items to cover the missing cash.
- Charging the customers more than the duplicate sales slips show and pocketing the difference.
- Misappropriating cash and charging the amounts taken to fictitious customers' accounts.

The following are some indications that one or more of your purchasing staff may be "on the take":

- Your company deals with only a handful of suppliers who do not change much. Most big jobs go to one or two firms.
- Final purchasing decisions are made by one person, with no technical staff to assess each purchase.
- The lifestyle of the purchasing executive is clearly more affluent than her or his salary would indicate.
- Purchasing files are not easily accessible or understandable.
- Many big orders are not covered by a single purchase order but are broken up into confusing elements, including changes and add-ons.
- There are no verified receiving reports.
- Reports from vendors that they cannot get a foot in the door are received (20% to 25% of your vendors should change annually).
- A buyer turns down a promotion that would move her or him to another department.

- Purchasing staffers come in early and leave late, and never take vacations.
- Costs have risen faster than what you know is the current inflation rate.

Manipulations to order processing systems can be accomplished by employees using any or all of the following:

- Unique off-line billing.
- Shipping items with values different than invoiced.
- Shipping at prices that are less than the minimum for a product shipped.
- Issuing credits for returned goods at prices higher than customers paid or for goods not returned.
- Closing out a product line.
- Open items charged to and paid by the wrong customer.
- Postponing payment of an invoice (forever) by placing items in a continuous float.

Losses from manipulations to accounts receivable systems can range from nickel and dime to tens of thousands of dollars. Some ways to manipulate receivables are misapplying checks, credit adjustments, wash sales, adjustments to customer journals, and truckload sales.

The following are ten commonly reported evidences of "management-directed" fraud in customer accounts receivable processing:

1. Preparing customer account statements that do not indicate existing credit balances.
2. Printing statements with proper credit balance entries but failing to send them to the customers involved.
3. Issuing a special report of "suppressed" customer account credit balances for use in handling subsequent inquiries and investigations.
4. Dropping all credit balances when the customer account has been inactive for one year.
5. Printing a code on customer account statements indicating that the credit balance has been "suppressed."
6. Retaining a credit balance in the customer account record until it appears certain that the customer will not request that it be refunded, . . . then writing it off.

7. Confusing various categories of charges and payments to distort the true nature of the amount owed by the customer—or owed to the customer.
8. Suppressing records of mistakes that favor customers, but always notifying them of mistakes not in their favor.
9. "Rounding off" all odd amounts against the customer.
10. Creating "administrative transactions" that remove credit balances without the knowledge of the customer.

Table 4–1 lists items that are conducive to fraud in both the organizational structure and its environment.

Table 4–1   Fraud-conducive Organizational Structures and Environments

Structure

- The business locations of the company are widely dispersed, key documents are created at outlying locations, and evidence as to material transactions must be obtained from more than one location.
- The company is highly diversified, having numerous different businesses, each with its own accounting system.
- Management is dominated by one or a few individuals.
- The company follows the practice of using different auditors for major segments.
- The company seems to need, but lacks, an adequate internal audit staff.
- Key financial positions, controller for example, do not seem to stay filled for very long.
- The company has no outside general counsel, using special counsel for individual matters; or outside general counsel seems to be switched with some frequency.
- The accounting and financial functions appear to be understaffed, resulting in constant crisis conditions.
- The audit closing requires substantive adjusting of entries.

Environment

- Lack of sufficient working capital and/or credit to continue the business.
- The urgent desire for a continued favorable earnings record in the hope of supporting the price of the company's stock.
- Massive demands for new capital in a developing industry and accordingly extreme competition therefore.
- Dependence on a single or relatively few products, customers, or transactions for the ongoing success of the venture.
- Little available tolerance on debt restrictions, such as maintenance of working capital and limits on additional permissible debt, or in complying with terms of revocable licenses necessary for the continuation of the business.
- The industry is declining or is characterized by a large number of business failures.
- Excess capacity has befallen the company (e.g., from the energy crisis).
- Existence of significant litigation, especially litigation between stockholders and management.
- Extremely rapid expansion of business or product lines.
- Numerous acquisitions, particularly as a diversification move.
- In accounts receivable, difficulties in collection from a class of customers (e.g., energy-related businesses, real estate investment trusts).
- Significant inventories, the physical qualities of which require evaluation not within the expertise of the auditor.
- A long-term manufacturing cycle for the company's products.
- Overly optimistic earnings forecasts.
- Significant obsolescence dangers because the company is in a high-tech industry.

5

Fraud In, Fraud Out

THE BASICS OF ACCOUNTING SYSTEMS

Accounting is simply the formalized recordkeeping of the financial transactions of a business. These transactions fall into logical groupings that are referred to as accounts. Accounts fall into five major categories—assets, liabilities, owner's equity, expenses, and income. Depending on the degree of sophistication of the accounting that is done by a particular company, these major categories are further broken down into the actual accounts—capital, sales, office supplies, salaries, raw materials, cash, and so on.

Each financial transaction that takes place affects at least two of these accounts, increasing one by the same amount the other is decreased by, so that the net effect is zero. In a simple accounting system, for example, the purchase of a typewriter decreases the Cash account and increases the Office Equipment and Sales Tax accounts; the sale of merchandise will decrease the Inventory account and increase either the Cash and Sales Discount accounts or the Accounts Receivable account. Ledgers are used to record each financial transaction as it occurs; summaries of these transactions are transferred to the appropriate accounts at the end of an accounting period, usually monthly. At this time, the books are balanced to ensure that the accounts "zero balance" in total; that is, that the company's Assets are equal to its Liabilities plus the Owner's Equity.

This ritual balancing only ensures that double-entry book-keeping has been maintained correctly for an entire accounting period; it does not ensure that the correct accounts have been increased and decreased. Only an audit can determine that a cash sale actually resulted in a decrease to the Inventory account and an increase to the Cash account.

Manual Accounting Systems

A manual accounting system requires handwritten entries of all financial transactions for a business. Source documents are forwarded to the bookkeeper who logs the transactions into the correct ledgers. Ledgers and accounts must be reconciled and balanced at least monthly. The accuracy and validity of input documents, as well as the correct posting of transactions, are the main controls that can be checked by an auditor.

Computerized Accounting Systems

Computerized accounting systems deal with large amounts of financial data, trying to replace the function of the bookkeeper in the posting, summing, and crossfooting of accounts. However, source documents, still the main form of input, are now forwarded to data entry instead of to the bookkeeper. Ledgers and accounts are now balanced "automatically" by the computer, usually more frequently than just at the end of the month. Again, the accuracy and validity of the source documents plus the correct functioning of the computer programs (the bookkeeper) are the main controls that can be checked by an auditor.

Similarities Between Systems

The similarities between a manual and a computerized accounting system begin with source documents—the sales tickets, expense records, and invoices of all business operations. In a manual system, these are forwarded directly to the bookkeeper for entry into the accounting books. Recognition of various types of transactions by the bookkeeper and translation into appropriate accounting entries is necessary to properly update the company's journals and ledgers.

In a computerized system, several routes may be used to get the account data into computerized files: documents could be forwarded to a data preparation area where they would be transformed into machine-readable form for computer processing; documents could be entered directly into the accounting system from a remote terminal; or, data could be generated by other computer systems such as a purchase order writing system. A computer program takes the place of the bookkeeper and records the accounting data into the Account Master File. The computer program, of course, must recognize different transaction types and post the information to the appropriate accounts.

A major difference between manual and computerized accounting systems is in the storage of Master Accounts. Records and summary accounts in a manual system are available in a human readable format (i.e., the "Books"). Each individual account can be scrutinized for content, and entries can be checked back to source documents. In the computerized system, the Books are stored on machine-readable, usually magnetic, storage devices. Deciphering the Books, therefore, requires transformation of this data back into human-readable formats. Checking original source documents to computer entries becomes difficult because of the transformations that the data has undergone in order to be first processed by the computer programs and then stored on the computer files.

The final process in any accounting system, manual or computerized, is consolidation and summarization of various accounts into financial reports and statements. In a manual system, this is accomplished by the bookkeeper using the journals and ledgers that make up the Books. In a computerized system, a computer program is needed to consolidate and present the bookkeeping information in the format required for financial reports and statements. The logic and processes the bookkeeper goes through in a manual system to prepare trial balances and working papers are paralleled in the computer program.

MONITORING COMPUTERIZED ACCOUNTING

Computers, in their management-assistance role, can provide instantaneous information necessary to monitor inventories, process orders, issue purchase orders, and bill customers. Although the computer can do all this and more, there is still the need for checks and controls of the computerized systems as well as the manual processes. These checks and controls are needed simply because it is humans that enter the initial data into the computer. And humans can and do make mistakes, and some people are prone to steal.

There can be no fully computerized system simply because someone—not a machine—must control, instruct, and feed data into the computer. The computer is, essentially, a logical but indiscriminate machine; that is, it does not question the data it receives (though it may reject it), and it simply follows instructions and turns out what it is told to turn out. It is the nature of the computer, how and why it operates with its human interface, that forces manual checks and controls. If incorrect data is put into the computer, it operates on the GIGO principle—Garbage In, Garbage Out. We need another acronym for criminal manipulation of the computer—FIFO, or Fraud In, Fraud Out.

The schematics in Appendix 5–1 attempt to show the interrelations between manual and computerized controls in an inventory system and how these controls can be audited. Although the use of computers is widespread, there are usually areas in any operation where manual intervention is necessary to complete the required processes. For example, in the Receiving department, a clerk may have to sight-verify the quantity of merchandise received and log this information on a receiving report document. Most audits of these functions are straightforward—is the clerk performing the necessary checks and logging the correct information? But what about the link from receiving report to computerized records? What about the computer program that is supposed to make sure that the amount received equals the amount ordered?

Just as easily as a receiving clerk can give "special" attention to preferred vendors, so can the computer programmer. Instructions can be generated so that edits are bypassed for "special" vendors; or for certain items, the balance-on-hand might be shorted in anticipation of later thefts. Whatever the technique, the result is the same—

serious losses for the company. That is why audits of computerized operations must be done as regularly as audits of manual operations.

Does the computer program actually perform its function? Does controlled input generate predictable output? Do output listings really reflect the processing that took place? Are all computer file updates logged for future audit requirements? For this example, of course, the final check is the verification that the manual system matches the computerized records—that is, does the physical inventory match the computerized inventory.

SUMMARY

Ignoring the need for auditing computerized processes is as dangerous as leaving the storeroom doors open—only the loss may be magnitudes greater. Just as the computer can process hundreds of normal transactions in a fraction of a minute, it can also generate hundreds of fraudulent transactions in the same amount of time.

APPENDIX 5–1

Controls and Audits in an Inventory System

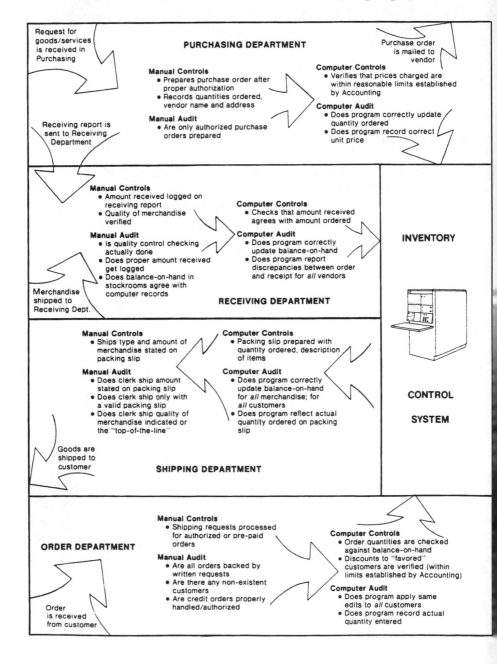

Request for goods/services is received in Purchasing

PURCHASING DEPARTMENT

Purchase order is mailed to vendor

Manual Controls
- Prepares purchase order after proper authorization
- Records quantities ordered, vendor name and address

Manual Audit
- Are only authorized purchase orders prepared

Computer Controls
- Verifies that prices charged are within reasonable limits established by Accounting

Computer Audit
- Does program correctly update quantity ordered
- Does program record correct unit price

Receiving report is sent to Receiving Department

Manual Controls
- Amount received logged on receiving report
- Quality of merchandise verified

Manual Audit
- Is quality control checking actually done
- Does proper amount received get logged
- Does balance-on-hand in stockrooms agree with computer records

Computer Controls
- Checks that amount received agrees with amount ordered

Computer Audit
- Does program correctly update balance-on-hand
- Does program report discrepancies between order and receipt for *all* vendors

INVENTORY

Merchandise shipped to Receiving Dept.

RECEIVING DEPARTMENT

Manual Controls
- Ships type and amount of merchandise stated on packing slip

Manual Audit
- Does clerk ship amount stated on packing slip
- Does clerk ship only with a valid packing slip
- Does clerk ship quality of merchandise indicated or the "top-of-the-line"

Computer Controls
- Packing slip prepared with quantity ordered, description of items

Computer Audit
- Does program correctly update balance-on-hand for *all* merchandise; for *all* customers
- Does program reflect actual quantity ordered on packing slip

CONTROL

SYSTEM

Goods are shipped to customer

SHIPPING DEPARTMENT

ORDER DEPARTMENT

Manual Controls
- Shipping requests processed for authorized or pre-paid orders

Manual Audit
- Are all orders backed by written requests
- Are there any non-existent customers
- Are credit orders properly handled/authorized

Computer Controls
- Order quantities are checked against balance-on-hand
- Discounts to "favored" customers are verified (within limits established by Accounting)

Computer Audit
- Does program apply same edits to *all* customers
- Does program record actual quantity entered

Order is received from customer

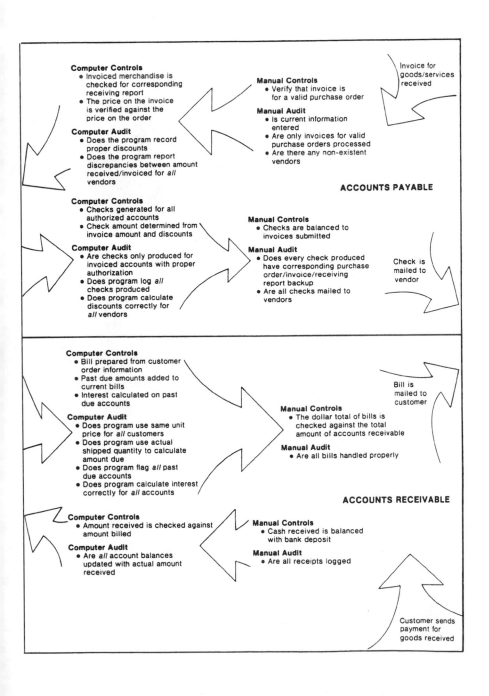

Computer Controls
- Invoiced merchandise is checked for corresponding receiving report
- The price on the invoice is verified against the price on the order

Computer Audit
- Does the program record proper discounts
- Does the program report discrepancies between amount received/invoiced for *all* vendors

Manual Controls
- Verify that invoice is for a valid purchase order

Manual Audit
- Is current information entered
- Are only invoices for valid purchase orders processed
- Are there any non-existent vendors

Invoice for goods/services received

ACCOUNTS PAYABLE

Computer Controls
- Checks generated for all authorized accounts
- Check amount determined from invoice amount and discounts

Computer Audit
- Are checks only produced for invoiced accounts with proper authorization
- Does program log *all* checks produced
- Does program calculate discounts correctly for *all* vendors

Manual Controls
- Checks are balanced to invoices submitted

Manual Audit
- Does every check produced have corresponding purchase order/invoice/receiving report backup
- Are all checks mailed to vendors

Check is mailed to vendor

Computer Controls
- Bill prepared from customer order information
- Past due amounts added to current bills
- Interest calculated on past due accounts

Computer Audit
- Does program use same unit price for *all* customers
- Does program use actual shipped quantity to calculate amount due
- Does program flag *all* past due accounts
- Does program calculate interest correctly for *all* accounts

Manual Controls
- The dollar total of bills is checked against the total amount of accounts receivable

Manual Audit
- Are all bills handled properly

Bill is mailed to customer

ACCOUNTS RECEIVABLE

Computer Controls
- Amount received is checked against amount billed

Computer Audit
- Are *all* account balances updated with actual amount received

Manual Controls
- Cash received is balanced with bank deposit

Manual Audit
- Are all receipts logged

Customer sends payment for goods received

6

The Legal Language of Fraud

To the ordinary layman, the words theft, fraud, embezzlement, larceny, and defalcation can be used somewhat interchangeably. Breach of trust or fiduciary responsibility, conversion, false representations, false pretenses, false tokens, false entries, and false statements are rarely used by laymen because they sound more ominous and legalistic. Yet the distinction between the former and the latter is that the words in the first set tend to be generic for a certain set of human behaviors and those in the second set are species of the first set.

The word with the broadest connotations in the above sets is *theft*. Most people have a sense of what that term means and implies. Even little children are wont to say and understand the implication of "You stole my toy." Translated that means "You took my toy without my permission and are keeping it from me against my will." Laws, perhaps, might be more respected and complied with if they were stated so simply. But alas, simplicity and laws do not mix.

While English teachers strive mightily to clarify and simplify, legislators make a habit of splitting hairs and complicating what is ordinary to disguise their lack of decisiveness or the political pressures of special-interest groups with whom they must interact for survival. Lawyers, being word technicians, then demand precision in language and will challenge new laws in which the draftsmanship leaves anything to be desired, because that is how they make their living. So there are a number of forces that seem to spend time squabbling about words and phrases and their meanings, thus making what was formerly understood intuitively, something which gets stated in such complex and long-winded terms that the ordinary layman can no longer understand even the simplest exhortation without counsel.

People can go to jail now just because they failed to seek counsel on a matter of statutory interpretation. As a layman, you are not free to interpret statutes unless you are willing to suffer the consequences of being wrong. Lawyers make a good deal of money issuing "opinion letters" to save you from jail—letters that say, if you do so and so, you will not violate the tax code, the securities laws, the labor laws, and so forth. In essence, lawyers can provide a good "cover" or excuse for the well heeled and better informed. After all, what would any "ordinary, reasonable prudent man" do under like or similar circumstances? You can always say, "I did the best I could. I sought the advice and counsel of Roscoe Replevin, a lawyer with impeccable credentials. He had a bad day and gave me some bum advice. So while I'm technically guilty, I had no evil intentions. Fine me if you will, but don't incarcerate me." And now, back to the issue of theft.

LEGAL DEFINITIONS OF THEFT AND FRAUD

"Theft" and "stealing" have become so generally understood and so commonly used that they are considered generic terms for a range of different crimes. The words themselves are rarely used in criminal statutes. The technical charge for the kind of behavior most of us think of as theft or stealing is called "larceny."

Larceny is usually defined as the wrongful taking and carrying away of the personal property of another with intent to convert it or

---

Note: For further explanation of the definitions in this chapter, see Black, Henry Campbell. *Black's Law Dictionary*, 4th ed. rev. and 5th ed., St. Paul: West, 1968 or 1979.

to deprive the owner of its use and possession (see Black, 1979, p. 792). If the taking is by stealth—surreptitiously—the crime committed is larceny. If the taking is by force or fear, the crime is robbery. If the taking is by guile and deception, by false representation, or concealment of that which should have been disclosed, the crime charged may be fraud.

Fraud, then, means any kind of artifice employed by one person to deceive another. Fraud is a generic term too. It embraces all the multifarious means that human ingenuity can conceive to get an unfair advantage over another—surprise, trick, cunning, false suggestion, or suppression of truth—as in the Watergate case.

Because of its generic use and application, the word *fraud* now means behavior that may be either criminal or civil, actionable or unactionable (*caveat emptor*—Let the buyer beware), or actual or constructive (by legal construction); and in a contractual sense, fraud may be found as the inducement for a contract or in the execution of a contract.

Embezzlement, which we have not discussed yet, is a "kissing cousin" of larceny and fraud. By definition, *embezzlement* is the fraudulent appropriation of property by a person to whom it has been entrusted, or into whose hands it has lawfully come (see Black, 1979, p. 468). It implies a breach of trust or fiduciary responsibility. Proving embezzlement has always been tough from a legal and language point of view. There is a story told in most law schools—usually in criminal law courses—of an ingenious lawyer who represented a bank teller charged with the crime of embezzlement. He very skillfully convinced the jury that his client may well have been guilty of larceny but certainly not embezzlement and that, technically, the crime charged was incorrect and his client should therefore be found innocent of that charge. So eloquent was his plea that the jury returned a not-guilty verdict. (See Chapter 8 for a discussion of embezzlement.)

Indignant at the loss, the prosecuting attorney then filed a complaint against the teller charging him with larceny. With a new jury and protection from the introduction of his remarks at the earlier trial, the defense lawyer just as eloquently convinced the jurors that, if anything, his client was guilty of embezzlement, certainly not the crime of larceny.

The major distinction between larceny and embezzlement lies in the issue of the legality of the custody of the article stolen. In larceny, the thief never has legal custody. He "feloniously took" the article from its owner. In embezzlement, the thief is legally authorized by its owner to take or receive the article and to possess it for a time. The formulation of intent to steal the article may occur subsequent to the time when it came into his or her possession or concurrently with initial possession. If initial possession and intent to steal occur simultaneously, the crime is larceny. If intent to steal occurs subsequent to initial possession, the crime is embezzlement. These hairsplitting distinctions make a prosecutor's life a mite harried and probably led to the creation of the bank teller story mentioned above.

But this book was not written for lawyers or teachers of English or even psychologists. It was written for people who have the burden of ferreting out fraud and documenting its existence—auditors, accountants, regulatory agents, investigators, and managers. What should they know about fraud, larceny, and embezzlement?

One thing they might want to know more about are definitions of the fraud species of crimes. The definitions given thus far are the broad range, generic, and common-law types of crimes (i.e., larceny, robbery, embezzlement, and criminal fraud). What are these fraud species types of crimes and how are they defined? They are as follows:

> *Deceit*—A fraudulent and cheating misrepresentation, artifice, or device, used by one or more persons, to deceive and trick another who is ignorant of the true facts, to the prejudice and damage of the party imposed on. *People v. Chadwick,* 143 Cal. 116 (Black, 1968).
>
> *Defalcation*—The act of a defaulter; misappropriation of trust funds or money held in any fiduciary capacity; failure to properly account for such funds. Usually spoken of officers of corporations or public officials. *In re Butts,* D.D. N.Y., 120 F. 970; *Crawford v. Burke,* 201 Ill. 581 (Black, 1968).
>
> *False and Misleading Statement*—Failure to state material fact made letter a "false and misleading statement" within rule of Securities and Exchange Commission. *SEC v. Okin,* C.C.A. N.Y., 132 F.2d 784, 787 (Black, 1968).
>
> *False Entry*—An entry in books of a bank or trust company that is intentionally made to represent what is not true or does not exist, which is intended either to deceive its officers or a bank examiner or to defraud the bank or trust company. *Agnew v. U.S.,* 165 U.S. 36 (Black, 1968).

False Pretenses—Designed misrepresentation of existing fact or condition whereby person obtains another's money or goods. (Example: giving a worthless check.) *People v. Gould*, 363 Ill. 348 (Black, 1968).

False Representation—A representation which is untrue, willfully made to deceive another to his or her injury.

False Statement—Under statutory provision, making it unlawful for an officer or director of a corporation to make any false statement with regard to corporation's financial condition. The phrase means something more than merely untrue or erroneous, but it implies that the statement is designed to be untrue and deceitful, and made with intention to deceive the person to whom false statement is made or exhibited. *State v. Johnston*, 149 S.C. 138 (Black, 1968).

False Token—In criminal law, a false document or sign of the existence of a fact; in general, used for the purpose of fraud. (Example: counterfeit money.)

Falsify—To counterfeit or forge; to make something false; to give a false appearance to anything. To make false by mutilation or addition: to tamper with; as to falsify a record or document. *Pov v. Ellis*, 66 Fla. 358 (Black, 1968).

Forgery—The false making or material altering, with intent to defraud, of anything in writing, which, if genuine, might apparently be of legal efficiency or the foundation of a legal liability. *People v. Routson*, 354 Ill. 573 (Black, 1968).

Fraudulent Concealment—The hiding or suppression of a material fact or circumstance that the party is legally or morally bound to disclose. *Magee v. Insurance Co.*, 92 U.S. 93 (Black, 1968).

Fraudulent Conversion—Receiving into possession money or property of another and fraudulently withholding, converting, or applying the same to or for one's own use and benefit, or to use and benefit any person other than the one to whom the money or property belongs. *Commonwealth v. Mitchneck*, 130 Pa. Super. 433 (Black, 1968).

Fraudulent or Dishonest Act—One which involves bad faith, a breach of honesty, a want of integrity, or moral turpitude. *Hartford Acc. and Indemn. Co. v. Singer*, 185 Va. 620 (Black, 1968).

Fraudulent Representation—1. A false statement as to material fact, made with intent that another rely thereon, which is believed by other party and on which he or she relies and by which he or she is induced to act and does act to his or her injury, and statement is fraudulent if speaker knows statement to be false or if it is made with utter disregard of its truth or falsity. (*Osborne v. Simmons*, Mo. App., 23 S.W.2d 1102.) 2. As a basis for law action, establishment of representation, falsity, scienter, deception, and injury is required. *Gray v. Shell Petroleum Corp.*, 212 Iowa 825 (Black, 1968).

Malfeasance—Evil doing; ill conduct; the commission of some act that is positively unlawful; the doing of an act that is wholly wrongful and unlawful; the doing of an act, which a person ought not to do at all, or the unjust performance of some act which the party had no right to do or which he or she had contracted not to do. Comprehensive term including any wrongful conduct that affects, interrupts, or interferes with the performance of official duties. State *ex rel. Knabb v. Frater*, 198 Wash. 675 (Black, 1968).

Misapplication—Improper, illegal, wrongful, or corrupt use or application of funds, property, etc. *Jewett v. U.S.*, C.C.A. Mass., 100 F. 841, 41 C.C.A. 88 (Black, 1968).

Misappropriation—The act of misappropriating or turning to a wrongful purpose; wrong appropriation; a term which does not necessarily mean peculation, although it may mean that. *Bannon v. Knauss*, 157 Ohio App. 228 (Black, 1968).

THE NEXT WAVE OF CORPORATE LITIGATION: ELECTRONIC DATA INTERCHANGE

A few hundred years ago business was conducted directly between buyers and sellers on a face-to-face basis. As businesses grew, buyers and sellers multiplied themselves through agents who also conducted business face-to-face. Then technology replaced face-to-face contact in the form of mail-order buying and selling, thanks to such retail giants as Sears-Roebuck, J.C. Penney, and Montgomery Ward. Telephone, telegraph, and cable ordering followed mail ordering. Now many firms do business by computer. The buzzword for this new form of buying and selling is Electronic Data Interchange, or EDI for short. Although we have made great progress in facilitating doing business between buyers and sellers, as we approach the twenty-first century, the law is still in the nineteenth century. We do have a Uniform Commercial Code (UCC) that incorporates large parts of the previous laws of sales, principals and agents, suretyship, bailments, and so on. But the UCC provides few insights on the rights and obligations of buyers and sellers who do business by computer. The UCC is technologically outdated.

At the moment, buying and selling by computer is done on the basis of trust between the parties, which means it is limited to customers or suppliers, or both, with whom a manufacturer has had longstanding business relationships. So the first security issue that must be addressed in EDI technology is legal. For example, what is the legal significance of an electronic purchase order transmitted by computer; an electronic invoice transmitted by computer; a digital signature on an order for payment or on a contract proposal; optically stored information; and digitized documents? Other legal questions are: When is a sale concluded? Where is a sale concluded? How can an electronic sale be repudiated or disavowed?

These questions have a bearing on the statute of limitations (when does the statute begin to run?), on the jurisdiction where suit should be brought if a contract is breached, and whether a contract between the parties exists at all. Most lawyers would, therefore, suggest a master contract be drafted and signed (in hard copy) between the parties before any electronic business is conducted. "Such a master contract would set out the rights, obligations, and liabilities of the transaction parties," says Palo Alto, California, attorney Fred Greguras of Fenwick, Stone, Davis & West.

Let us consider an industry deeply committed to EDI and survey a few other risks. Because Detroit is my hometown and current place of residence, I have more than a casual interest in the auto industry. What auto companies and their suppliers (and dealers) have been doing a lot lately is linking their computers for purposes of better quality control, inventory management, and production scheduling. The basic purpose of these innovations is labor, material, and distribution cost reduction. But higher quality and better customer service are major benefits too. Therefore, you will not find many critics of this growing technology in or around Detroit. Indeed, Detroit hopes to become a leading center for EDI technology.

Roger Caderet, a veteran EDI planner and designer at General Motors in Detroit and now with Ernst and Young & Co., specializing in EDI consulting, says three serious problems—legal, audit, and security—face any organization that intends to implement EDI technology. We have discussed a few of the legal issues; however, audit and security issues cry for their own treatment.

EDI presents some risks that are significantly different from a standalone computer or a dedicated system. Once outside access is permitted, the host system should be reconfigured from a security standpoint. The best way to begin is to undertake a security risk assessment of the intended EDI system. What risk categories should be analyzed? Physical security? Proprietary information protection? Yes, all of them. The basic concerns here are threats such as data or system destruction and damage, data disclosure and modification, processing delays, and denial of services. Threats that should be anticipated include the following:

- Fires
- Heavy rains, high winds, and lightning that could cause water and storm damage
- Hardware and software malfunction
- HVAC, power, and communications failure
- Contaminants such as dust, smoke, and noxious gas
- Electromagnetic interference and static discharge
- System (building and/or computer) crashes
- Forced physical entry
- Electronic intrusions
- Employee compromise, fraud, theft, embezzlement, and misuse of resources
- Errors of all kinds—input, thruput, output, and transmission

Indeed, realistically, you should expect loss of data when implementing EDI (as with other major systems innovations); therefore, backup and recovery should be a part of the implementation and operational plan. Here are some other thoughts: (1) critically review the software you intend to use for EDI before its adoption, and (2) know the software's limitations and compensate or make allowances for these limitations.

Currently, EDI runs on the basis of trust between manufacturers, suppliers, customers, and/or dealers. To maximize its cost-reduction capabilities, EDI creates many databases, accessible by many people for many purposes. Typical access-control features for individual EDI users include (1) terminal and user IDs (passwords, coded cards, electronic signatures, physical characteristics—fingerprints, retina scans, and so on), (2) user profits (e.g., user behavior characteristics and normal patterns of use), and (3) user authorization limits. These control measures are intended to restrict access to those persons with preestablished needs and to limit even those persons to data that are vital to the proper discharge of their job-related duties. The controls are also intended to monitor, flag, and log exceptions to security rules. Data security personnel need to review logs and follow-up on breaches of security. Table 6–1 summarizes what the authors consider some EDI risks and their remedies.

Electronic data interchange, a wave of the future technology among manufacturing firms and their suppliers or customers, may have some propensity for error. Robert Fisher, president of an EDI development firm (Foresight Corporation), says that 80 percent of EDI users (or about 8,000 firms) are experiencing growing pains that undermine reliability and accuracy (*Network World*, 9-17-90).

Heralded for some years as the application wave of the future for order processing, inventory management, and purchase order or payables or both, EDI is finally coming on strong, despite legal, audit, and security risks inherent in the technology. *Computerworld* (5-15-90, p. 10) says the most common applications of EDI today are "shipment status requests, order placement, billing, bank cash reporting and e-mail."

Table 6–1   EDI Risks and Remedies

Risks	*Remedies*
Service interruption	Backup and recovery planning
Transmission interception	Cryptography
Electronic intrusion	Data access and authorization controls
Forced entry	Physical access controls
Data disclosure	Information classification and dissemination controls
Data modification	Data accuracy and exceptions reporting controls
Embezzlement	Separation of duties and audit trails
Employee sabotage	Rewarding work environment
Insider/outsider collusion	Depends on how much authority and knowledge insider has. High levels of both would make it difficult to detect.
Legality of EDI transactions	Master contract between the parties in the network; new legislation

Network World (5-22-89, p. 17) says the retail industry believes EDI to be a valuable tool for monitoring inventory levels. Sales are tracked by Uniform Product Codes (UPC) on price tags. The data are then fed into an in-store controller that updates the inventory by communicating with a host computer. When stock falls below certain levels, the host automatically sends a purchase order to suppliers. Retailers expect that this "quick-response" technology will save them millions of dollars by decreasing distribution, administrative, merchandise, and inventory storage costs.

Texas Instruments, Inc., says it will soon get its phone bills via EDI, and colleges are moving toward exchanging transcripts by EDI (*Network World*, 5-15-89). The EPA is exploring the feasibility of accepting reports from regulated companies by way of EDI; the U.S. government's GSA issued a regulation allowing federal agencies to accept billing and payment data from transportation carriers by EDI; but, corporate funds transfers, a subset of EDI, are not mushrooming, however. Only 2.5 percent of U.S. and Canadian corporations use EDI (*Computerworld*, 5-15-89).

The litigation potential of EDI has to do, not with its flaws or weaknesses, but with its strengths. Many private- and public-sector employers have used EDI to reduce costs. EDI has done so very well, but at a heavy social cost (i.e., unemployment, contract cancellations with small suppliers). Human tragedies may set off a tidal wave of lawsuits for contract breaches, discrimination, and unfair business practices. EDI implementors also should be prepared for employee sabotage, theft, and disclosure of proprietary information. Although EDI will produce a fair amount of risk to its adopters, electronic funds transfer systems theft could be an even more serious security problem.

Note: Portions of this chapter have been excerpted from *Computer Security Digest*, 1989 and 1990 issues.

7

On-the-Job Thievery: Common Schemes of the Working Person

To work successfully for long periods of time, internal theft schemes must be simple, quick to execute, and involve small amounts of money or merchandise at any one time. These schemes, in essence, must fool or override internal control mechanisms that accountants design to detect them. Control mechanisms consist mainly of setting predefined limits of authority over expenditures, asset acquisitions, and job-related duties. It is truly amazing how ingenious relatively uneducated on-the-job thieves are in circumventing control mechanisms designed by people of much higher intellect. A determined thief can find weak links in controls faster than a hungry dog can find the sausage section of a meat counter.

What is this peculiar twist of mind that "low-brow" thieves have that pits them successfully against the best brains money can buy? First, they do not want to be caught, which gives them an edge in sheer deviousness and creativity. Second, their simple minds look for weaknesses in controls. They do not attack frontally, but at the flanks or behind the lines. Disguise and surprise are their main battle strategies.

Theft on-the-job is largely a counterculture phenomenon. It pits the powers that be against the young and the lowly in income and social status. And, because the young and the lowly are more numerous, have less financial security, and, ergo, more economic need, their schemes are often ingenious and cooperatively developed. Although no one member of the subculture may have power to override controls, they can do so collectively, or creatively by feigning emergencies during which controls are temporarily dispensed with.

BASIC PRINCIPLES OF SCAMS

Internal theft scams work on the basis of four principles: (1) disguise, (2) divergence, (3) diversion, and (4) conversion. *Disguise* means masking identities, activities, authorities, and transactions so that they have the appearance of legitimacy. A *divergence* is a departure from a norm; a deviation. Internal controls are norms, as mentioned before. To carry on a successful theft, the divergence must not appear to be so; it must be masked or disguised or made to look normal. *Diversion* means distracting or relaxing. In a military context, it means drawing the enemy's attention away from a planned point of attack. A *conversion*, legally, is an unauthorized act that deprives an owner of his or her property permanently or for an indefinite time.

Here are several illustrations of scams that have plagued businesses for years:

- Cash conversions
- Receivables conversions
- Inventory conversions
- Accounts payable diversions

How do employees convert cash, receivables, or inventory? (Oh, let me count the ways!) There is no limit to ingenuity when it comes to theft and conversion of assets. The last chapter of that book will never be written. But, here are a few simple ideas that have worked in the past.

Cash Conversions

Cash conversions occur mainly when too much authority or responsibility is vested in one person (inadequate separation of duties). If one person (1) opens the mail and accounts for incoming receipts, (2) makes bank deposits, (3) reconciles monthly bank statements, (4) records sales and receipts on accounts receivable, (5) issues credit memos to customers, and (6) is the petty cash fund custodian, you may have the worst of all worlds. Look for all the following schemes in such an environment:

- Diversion of petty cash for personal use by submitting fictitious documentation (phony expense bills, invoices, meal chits).
- "Borrowing" from the petty cash fund and using fictitious or personal checks to keep the account balance in line—a not uncommon offense by petty cash custodians.
- Deposit lapping—"borrowing" cash from funds to be deposited on the theory that you will make it up on the next day (if your horse comes in!).
- On the disbursement side of cash accounting, you can "kite" checks; that is, establish two or more checking accounts in other federal reserve districts. When the main account is low, draw a check on one of the other accounts, deposit it to the main account, and while the kited check is in the process of clearing, make a deposit so that funds are in the account when the kited check comes back through the clearinghouse. (In this electronic age, the ability to use kited checks may become impossible.)

Receivables Conversion

Lapping of accounts receivable is another common scam. If you are handling customer receipts and some pay in cash, you can have a field day for a while at least. Lapping receivables involves taking the payment of customer A (who pays in cash) and waiting until the next day to give the company credit; that is, when you take customer B's money and apply it to customer A's account. Now customer B is short changed, so you wait until day three, when more money comes in and then you credit customer B with the money you get from customer C. A handful of bookkeepers and bank tellers have played this game for years. And, even with computers and point of sale terminals, the scam goes on. Technology has not deferred, deterred, nor even detected this type of fraud. (But some progress is being made in "flagging" transactions that appear unusual (e.g., out of range or inconsistent with a pre-identified bookkeeper/user's pattern of transaction processing).

Inventory Conversions

Although cash and receivables scams mainly involve clerical or white-collar workers, inventory conversions mainly involve blue-collar factory and warehouse employees, truck drivers, and, sometimes, even company vendors who corrupt these people. The number, variety, and complexity of inventory scams are impossible to estimate, assess, or catalog. The design of such scams is a never-ending process. The following are but a few possibilities:

- Arbitrarily reclassifying inventory to a "no" value or limited value category (e.g., damaged, obsolete, sample, "freebie," back-ordered, reshipment of lost or misdelivered goods, a substitute for out-of-stock goods previously paid for by a customer, and so on).
- Undercounted goods on the receiving side; overcounted goods on the shipping side of the warehouse.
- Throwing perfectly good material into a dumpster and later reclaiming it when no one else is around.
- Accepting short weights or counts from a salvage operator who has contracted to buy scrap from the plant at higher-than-competitive prices—then, splitting the ill-gotten proceeds.

Accounts Payable Diversion (Disbursement Frauds)

Any clerk who processes payment claims for purchased materials or services, benefits or payroll, refunds, rebates, and discounts can have a rewarding career if his or her financial needs are great and personal resources are scarce. It also helps if his or her ethics are low and internal controls are weak.

Disbursement scams are the most common of all employee thefts and embezzlements. In theory, if controls are tight, this fraud should never occur. But because accounts and claims payable clerks do not usually handle cash money, we often fail to realize that access to cash in a physical sense is not the only criteria. If I can get my hands on anything that can be easily converted into cash (e.g., claims benefit forms, vendor invoice forms, and so on), I can get cash. All it takes is a little subterfuge, such as forgery, counterfeiting, and false pretense, and a fatal flaw in control mechanisms.

A common flaw in accounts payable processing in a computerized environment is allowing an accounts payable clerk access to the vendor master file to add or delete names (a separation of duties problem). In the usual case of such frauds, the clerk fabricates the name of a vendor, often a service provider (e.g., janitorial, maintenance, consultant) and adds the name to the master file of approved vendors. Then, the name is recorded in the assumed name file in the county seat, a post office box is rented, a bank account is established, and pads of invoices are printed up. The clerk makes up a fake invoice, forges approval authorities, and orders the system to generate a check payable to the phony vendor. This scam can go on for years if the clerk does not become too greedy, tip his or her hand by high living, or start to behave in a bizarre manner.

How to Detect Embezzlement

THE HIGH COST OF EMBEZZLEMENT

Embezzlers steal $4 billion to $6 billion a year from their employers. Yet their thefts are said to be rarely detected. If detected, their crimes are rarely prosecuted; and, if prosecuted, their sentences are very light. Indeed, embezzlers may even raise more havoc for public accountants than they do for their employers in the sense that so many embezzlements result in civil litigation for negligence brought by hapless client victims against their auditors for not detecting the embezzlement sooner.

PROFILING THE TYPICAL EMBEZZLER

Who are these embezzlers, and what makes them behave the way they do? In the literature of criminology, the classic definition of an *embezzler* is someone who holds a position of trust and finds himself or herself with an unshareable problem, usually of a financial nature, that can be resolved by "borrowing" the funds of an employer. ("Borrowing" usually is a rationalization.) There are a few other characteristics as well. Embezzlers tend to have low self-esteem or compulsive personalities (i.e., gamble, drink, or eat excessively) and have expensive lifestyles or hobbies, or both. Generally, they are also said to commit their acts of defalcation alone, over extended periods of time, and in increasing amounts before they are apprehended. Usually embezzlers do not make "one grand hit" for a million dollars and then run away; they are not "hit-and-run" criminals like confidence men and women are.

HOW EMBEZZLEMENT SURFACES

Evidence of employee embezzlement surfaces initially in one of the following ways:

- An accounting discrepancy, irregularity, questionable transaction, or asset loss is detected in the course of routine internal, external, operational, or compliance audit.
- A complaint or allegation of misconduct is made by corporate insiders (e.g., the employee's peers, subordinates, or superiors).
- A complaint or allegation of misconduct is made by corporate outsiders (e.g., suppliers, contractors, customers, competitors, police, security, or regulatory officials and friends, associates, or relatives of the employee).
- There is a noticeable change in the behavior of the suspected culprit.

Detection of embezzlement* is possible through (1) the traditional control concepts of separation of duties and audit trails, (2) periodic financial and operational audits, (3) the gathering of intelligence on the lifestyles and personal habits of employees, (4) allegations and complaints of fellow employees, (5) the logging of exceptions to prescribed controls and procedures, (6) the review of variances in operating performance expectations (standards, goals, objectives, budgets, plants), (7) the intuition of the embezzler's superiors, and (8) generalized suspicion.

---

*Some of the materials that follow have been abstracted from several of the author's previous works (i.e., Bologna, *Fraud Auditing and Forensic Accounting*, John Wiley & Sons, New York, 1987; Bologna, *Corporate Fraud*, Butterworth-Heinemann, Boston, 1983; and various issues of the *Forensic Accounting Review* published by CPSI, Plymouth, Michigan.

Each embezzler also has a pattern of theft that is somewhat unique but discernible to an experienced fraud auditor; that is, an account category that gets an inordinate amount of "padding" to cover up the loss, a particular step in the audit trail procedures that often gets bypassed, circumvented, or overridden; a fake supplier or contractor whose account balance gets manipulated; an input document that often is fabricated, counterfeited, or forged. Most long-term embezzlement schemes, after discovery, are found to be very simple.

Embezzlement Methods

Cash disbursement embezzlement is the most common fraud in books of account, generally involving the creation of fake documents or false entries, or both, in some category of expense (e.g., purchases or payroll—usually in the form of a phony invoice from a phantom supplier or a faked time card from a phantom employee). The fabricated purchases may be for merchandise, raw materials, repairs, maintenance, janitorial or temporary help, insurance, travel and entertainment, benefits, and so forth. Fabricating the purchase of raw material and merchandise is tough to accomplish because costs of manufacture and sale are closely scrutinized by top management. If the fabricated purchases are for service or supplies rather than merchandise or raw material, the fraud is easier to execute and conceal. These expenses are not monitored as closely as manufacturing and sales costs.

Cash disbursement frauds are very common in small firms with one-person accounting departments or in situations in which separation of duties and audit trails are weak or nonexistent. Computerization of small firms exacerbates the disbursement fraud problem because small business owners are too trusting of data generated by computer.

Cash receipts frauds are also common in small businesses. The common, classic cash receipts fraud involves the lapping of cash or accounts receivable, or both; that is, "borrowing" from today's sales or receipts and replacing them with tomorrow's sales or receipts. In either event, the fraud requires the creation of fake data, fake reports, and/or false entries. There are several other receipts' frauds of note. *Skimming* is holding out or intercepting some of the proceeds of cash sales before any entry is made of their receipt. This is also called "fraud on the front-end."

Another form of receivables fraud can be generated by the issuance of fake credits for discounts, refunds, rebates, or returns and allowances. Here, a conspiracy, with a customer who shares the proceeds of the fake credit with an insider, may be required.

High-Level versus Low-Level Embezzlers

Embezzlers are persons who hold positions of trust; that is, they have ready access to books, records, cash, and other assets. Embezzlers are not, however, exclusively bookkeepers or accountants. Indeed, embezzlers hold jobs at all levels, from top management to nonmanagement personnel. Their theft schemes are as many and varied as they themselves are. Although payables frauds are the most common frauds committed by people in accounting roles, faking debits and credits knows no bounds. Every account category—such as cash, receivables, inventory, purchases, payables, payroll, contracted services, supplies, GS&A expenses, and so on—is vulnerable.

THE CRIME OF EMBEZZLEMENT

By legal definition, *embezzlement* is the "fraudulent appropriation of property by a person to whom it has been entrusted, or to whose hands it has lawfully come" (Black, 1968/1979). It implies a breach of trust or fiduciary responsibility.

Larceny usually is defined as the "wrongful taking and carrying away of the personal property of another with intent to convert it or to deprive the owner of its use and possession" (Black, 1968 and 1979). If the taking is through stealth—surreptitiously—the crime committed is larceny. If the taking is through force of fear, the crime committed is robbery. If the taking is through guile and deception, through false representation, or through concealment of that which should have been disclosed, the crime charged may be fraud.

The major distinction between larceny and embezzlement lies in the issue of the legality of custody of the article stolen. In larceny, the thief never had legal custody; he or she "feloniously took" the article stolen. In embezzlement, the thief is legally authorized by the owner to take or receive the article and to possess it for a time. The formulation of intent to steal the article may occur subsequent to the time when it came into his or her possession or concurrently with initial possession. If initial possession and intent to steal occur simultaneously, the crime is larceny. If intent to steal occurs subsequent to initial possession, the crime is embezzlement.

The Embezzlement Environment

Embezzlement, like all crimes, is a product of motive and opportunity. Embezzlement motives include economic (need of greed), egocentric (showing off), ideological (revenge), and psychotic (obsessive-compulsive behavior). Opportunity is created through the absence of internal controls or through weaknesses in internal controls. Motives and opportunities play off against one another. The greater the opportunity, the less the motive to need to steal. The greater the motive, the less the opportunity. The following control environment factors enhance the probability of embezzlement:

- Inadequate rewards
- Inadequate internal controls
- No separation of duties or audit trails
- Ambiguity in job roles, duties, responsibilities, and areas of accountability
- Failure to counsel and take administrative action when performance levels or personal behaviors fall below acceptable levels
- Inadequate operational reviews—lack of timely or periodic audits, inspections, and follow-up to ensure compliance with company goals, priorities, policies, procedures, and governmental regulations
- Other motivational issues:
    - Inadequate orientation and training on legal, ethical, and security issues
    - Inadequate company policies with respect to sanctions for legal, ethical, and security breaches
    - Failure to monitor and enforce policies on honesty and loyalty

Proving Criminal Intent in Embezzlement Cases

Without a voluntary and full confession, proving "criminal intent" in white-collar crime cases is the most formidable challenge to the skills and patience of investigators and auditors, primarily because evidence of such intent is usually circumstantial. You rarely have direct proof of a defendant "knowingly" or "willfully" violating larceny, embezzlement, or fraud laws. Such intent has to be inferred from other facts, such as the defendant's education, training, experience, intelligence; sophistication in the ways of business, finance, or accounting; past actions; past contradictory statements; tacit admissions; efforts to conceal records; efforts to destroy evidence; evidence of subornation of perjury or obstruction of justice; and evidence of conversion of funds to one's own use.

Defense lawyers in criminal cases often direct their whole defense to the issue of criminal intent because it is so difficult to prove. In the era of modern business, criminal intent is also complex, so much so that reasonable doubt can be created by a clever attorney. So how does one go about proving intent beyond a reasonable doubt?

As noted before, evidence of education, experience, training, intelligence, and sophistication in the ways of business, finance, and accounting may bear on the issue of generalized intent (i.e., knowledge, willfulness, and evil motive). However, some laws have specific intent requirements. As discussed previously, larceny, for example, is the taking and carrying away of the personal property of another with the intention of permanently depriving him or her of its use. Intending to "borrow" may not meet that statutory element of proof.

Take the example of the proverbial bookkeeper/embezzler who uses an accounts receivable lapping scheme. The bookkeeper has some limited right to access certain assets of the employer and the responsibility to make certain entries in the business records of the firm. In need of money to pay a gambling speculation debt, high living, or family medical problems, the bookkeeper decides to "borrow" $1,000. A customer's check payable to the company is received. The bookkeeper opens the mail, finds customer A's check for $1,000, substitutes it for $1,000 in the cash drawer, intending to make an entry crediting the receipt to customer A's account the next day when another $1,000 check is expected from customer B; then, customer B's check is used for covering customer A's account. The subsidiary ledger account of customer A shows that payment was made. But the control account audit does not reflect the receipt. An audit might disclose the discrepancy in accounts receivable and in the cash drawer at that point. One further step might be taken to conceal the defalcation. If the bookkeeper can access a credit memo form and can pretend authority to issue same by a forgery, customer A's account could be written off fictitiously as a discount, a rebate, allowance, or even a bad debt. That effort at concealment would bear on the issue of intent or be used to rebut the bookkeeper's defense or lack of intent to embezzle.

Such evidence alone, however, may not be enough to convict the bookkeeper of embezzlement, nor would evidence of high living, gambling, speculation, and family expense prove intent per se. That kind of evidence, however, would provide a motive for embezzlement and would be admissible for that purpose. Evidence of the improper entries alone do not prove intent. The bookkeeper may claim in defense that his or her intention was not to permanently deprive the employer of the money, just the "borrowing" thereof.

Evidence of this kind of borrowing implies or infers an intention to breach a fiduciary responsibility, which could help to prove criminal intent in an embezzlement case, if not in larceny. Individually, these pieces of evidence may not be enough to convict, but when joined together, they might. For example, the following facts may prove intent beyond a reasonable doubt:

- The bookkeeper is educated, trained, and experienced in accounting.
- The bookkeeper has a fiduciary responsibility to keep and maintain records in a timely and accurate manner.
- The bookkeeper has been employed by the company in that capacity for at least five years and knows the company's accounting policies, procedures, controls, and how to make proper entries.
- The bookkeeper's living expenses exceed his or her income by several orders of magnitude.
- The bookkeeper was fired from two previous jobs when large amounts of money in his or her custody were found missing.
- The lapping scheme went on for three years and the bookkeeper kept a running tab of "borrowings." He or she now claims the running tab proves his or her intention to repay. In a barroom conversation a year ago, however, he or she told an acquaintance that the company could be "stolen blind" by a clever thief because its controls were so weak.
- When the cash drawer was counted during the audit and investigation, a check from the bookkeeper to the company for a large

sum of money that was used to balance the drawer was found. It equaled the amount of the embezzlement for the current year.
- Evidence exists of concealment of documents, destruction of records, forged signatures, counterfeited documents, false statements, and solicitation of false testimony.

When these facts are added together, a judge or jury may reasonably conclude that the defendant indeed did formulate criminal intent.

THE AUDITOR'S DUTY TO DETECT FRAUD, THEFT, AND EMBEZZLEMENT

The responsibility for detecting transaction and financial reporting fraud has not been warmly accepted by outside auditors. Despite their protestations, many courts have suggested independent auditors have such a duty. These precedents have been established in situations in which outside auditors have been sued in stockholder class-action suits, by regulatory agencies, and by clients. The essence of the charge in these suits is that outside auditors have a duty to detect fraud in books of account, at least to the point in which clients have actively attempted to deceive them by concealing fraudulent transactions or entries.

A large number of professional malpractice suits against outside auditors involve allegations of undetected embezzlement. Some of the distinguishing characteristics in such malpractice suits follow:

- Most businesses involved are nonpublic, small, family-owned enterprises
- A company with a one-person, unbonded bookkeeping staff and loose internal controls
- A company with poor prospects of business survival and a chronic cash flow shortage
- A company with inactive or incompetent management and a high rate of turnover of outside audit firms
- The engagement most often involves a review or compilation rather than certified statements

Financial Auditing versus Fraud Auditing

Financial auditing is a methodology intended to evaluate the level of accuracy, timeliness, and completeness of the recordings of business transactions. Auditors, however, do not review all transactions. Tests of accuracy, timeliness, and completeness are accomplished by sampling and confirmation techniques. The purpose of such testing is to determine whether transaction data are free of material error and financial statements are accordingly free of material misstatement.

Fraud auditing, although borrowing many techniques from financial auditing, is more of a mind-set than a methodology. It relies on creativity (right-brain thinking) as much as it does on reasoning (left-brain thinking). Indeed, it requires that the fraud auditor think (not act) like a thief; that is, where are the weakest links in the chain of controls? How can controls be attacked without drawing attention? How can a thief destroy the evidence of an attack? What powers does he or she have that can be enlarged? What plausible explanation can be given if someone is suspicious of his or her activities? If apprehended, how can he or she explain away the conduct? The more a fraud auditor can learn to think like a thief, the better his or her effort to detect fraud. (See Chapter 1 for more details on fraud.)

Financial and fraud auditing also differ in the degree of concern for evidence of material error or misstatement. Although the materiality rule in financial auditing has its place in a cost-benefit context, materiality is not a guiding principle in fraud auditing. The amount of visible fraud may be small, but frauds in books of account can be like icebergs—the biggest part is below the surface. Discovering even small discrepancies can surface large defalcations. That is one reason why auditors often say they discover fraud by accident, not by audit plan or design. In truth, the "discovery" of fraud is generally no accident. It comes from diligent effort and a basic assumption by an auditor that if fraud is there, he or she is determined to find it. A fraud auditor needs the following skills:

- Reconstructing financial transactions through third-party sources
- Gathering and preserving accounting evidence for trial
- Testifying as an expert witness
- Calculating net worth and living expenses
- Inspecting documents for authenticity, alteration, forgery, and counterfeiting
- Documenting a fraud case for criminal, civil, and insurance claim purposes

- Designing fraud scenarios, such as imagining what a criminal might think and might do in situations in which internal controls are loose or are not enforced and the criminal has certain powers and authority over assets and accounting records

What is it that most distinguishes fraud auditors from financial auditors? In most respects, they are the same. The financial auditor is in his or her element when books and records are complete and reasonably accurate. The fraud auditor must make order of what appears to be chaos in books and records. Most of the supporting documents the fraud auditor must access for confirmation are in the hands of third parties who may not be inclined to assist in the audit effort.

Fraud auditors tend to be right-brain thinkers; that is, more creative in thought processes. In that context, they may better understand the inner working of the criminal mind because criminals are not noted for orderly, rational, or systematic thinking. Many criminals neither plan their crimes thoroughly nor anticipate the consequences of being caught. Most embezzlers, on the other hand, steal small sums for an extended period of time.

Detecting Employee Fraud, Theft, and Embezzlement

How does one go about detecting and proving employee fraud, theft, and embezzlement given the fact that an element of these crimes is intentional deception or concealment (i.e., hiding, destroying, or altering evidence of the crime)? Detecting such crimes can take the form of noting financial discrepancies and exceptions or what accountants call errors and irregularities. Errors and irregularities can take the form of intentional breaches of generally accepted accounting principles or the creation of fictional accounts, amounts, and transactions, to say nothing of simple mistakes such as misclassified accounts and posting errors. Exceptions may include transactions and amounts that seem at variance with expectations (i.e., too high; too low; too often; too rare; odd times, places, and people).

These cases can also surface from inside and outside sources. For example, allegations and complaints of criminal conduct may be made by work associates, vendors, customers, and stockholders.

Other methods of detecting such crimes include observation and intelligence gathering. An employee with a weakness for alcohol, gambling, sex, or expensive living habits may become suspect if those behaviors interfere with work performance.

Detecting and proving employee fraud, theft, and embezzlement is therefore a matter of knowledge, skills, attitude, and experience. The knowledge base of persons involved in detecting and proving crimes includes accounting, legal, and investigation principles. Necessary skills are: auditing; interrogation; locating missing witnesses, documents, and assets; testifying as an expert witness; anticipating defenses; conducting searches for evidence; and so on. The attitudinal component requires that a person involved in investigating, auditing, and trying such cases be self-confident, dogged, tireless, open-minded, and fair.

Experience means a disciplined and experiential connection with the field for some time—first as an apprentice under a mentor, then as journeyman or senior. Few "masters" are actively involved in investigating, auditing, and prosecuting this kind of white-collar crime. The persons in the field are learning new things every day. Indeed, they must; deceit and dishonesty take on new forms every day.

PREVENTING EMPLOYEE FRAUD, THEFT, AND EMBEZZLEMENT

Preventing employee fraud, theft, and embezzlement is thought to be a simple matter of installing and maintaining tight accounting controls like separating duties (receiving cash versus recording cash receipts) and audit trails (a chain of supporting documents that prove a transaction is valid). But accounting controls alone cannot do the entire job of prevention. Poor controls provide opportunities to steal, defraud, or embezzle. The inspiration, however, comes from the psyches of the thieves, which provide the motivation. Motivation is effected by need, greed, and corruption, among other things. Motivation is both a personal thing and a group thing. If an employee is a happy, loyal, and productive team member, there is not much inspiration to steal or cheat.

To avoid or prevent employee theft, fraud, and embezzlement, a climate of trust, honesty, and cooperation should be established.

How is that done? A climate of trust, honesty, and cooperation can be established if top management role-models those values in its own behaviors or interactions with employees. A bit of regular, periodic security-orientation training will help too. (See Chapter 7 for a discussion of some common embezzlement schemes.)

EMBEZZLEMENT BY COMPUTER: THE UNCONVENTIONAL WISDOM

The conventional wisdom in manual accounting circles suggests the threat of embezzlement can be reduced by implementing good internal controls (e.g., segregation of duties and audit trails). In computerized accounting circles, conventional wisdom suggests that the key to embezzlement reduction in these systems is to distribute controls along with the application (Perry, 1984). The conventional wisdom in criminology suggests the threat of embezzlement is further reduced by hiring people in positions of trust who do not have unshareable financial burdens (Cressey, 1953).

These theories seem to say that embezzlement is a product of opportunity (easy access to funds and inadequate internal controls) and motive (economic need or perhaps greed). There is another body of knowledge that suggests a third causation: the culture or moral climate of the employer organization (Deal & Kennedy, 1982).

The culture of an organization is composed of its corporate values, beliefs, heroes, rites, and rituals. The risk of embezzlement may be heightened in corporate cultures in which economic values predominate (i.e., short-term profits, fat bonuses, plush trappings for offices). The senior management of such firms, acting as role models, encourage subordinates to buy into their values. If success is merely an economic thing, why shouldn't everyone have a shot at it? If it cannot be achieved legally or ethically, well then what is wrong with a little lying, cheating, and stealing? "There is a little dishonesty in everyone's heart" (Jaspan & Black, 1980).

Although corporate crime and occupational crime (i.e., embezzlement) both may be white-collar crimes, they are otherwise not comparable (Clinard & Yeager, 1980). But the policies of some corporations can encourage the "criminal tendencies" of particular executives (Clinard & Yeager, 1980, p. 58).

PC Use and Embezzlement in Small Businesses

The rise in use of personal computers (PCs) for accounting purposes has some untoward side effects. In earlier times, the control concepts of separation of duties and paper trails discouraged the commission of embezzlement in large firms. But in small businesses, with unsophisticated systems and personnel, these controls often did not exist. One person was assigned all or most accounting functions, including cash handling, bank reconciliations, and check disbursements, as well as the posting of receivables to subsidiary ledgers. Embezzlement was a high risk and a continuous threat. Over the years, as theories of control made their way even into small businesses, the threat was reduced. The microcomputer has brought us back to square one.

The use of PCs in small businesses for accounting applications has zoomed. The low cost of hardware and software for accounting purposes makes PCs available even to Mom-and-Pop stores. In most of these small enterprises, one person does all the accounting on a PC—without oversight from anyone. There is no separation of duties and very little in the way of an audit trail. It is an open invitation to embezzlement. Given these realities, it is also far more difficult to detect and document embezzlement in the microenvironment. Table 8–1 lists some of the factors that enhance the probability of discovering internal theft, fraud, and embezzlement by computer.

AVOIDING LIABILITY SUITS BY CLIENT/VICTIMS OF EMBEZZLEMENTS

The following are a few suggestions to avoid the cost and embarrassment of client litigation:

- Auditors should be circumspect about suing clients for fees. Such suits are generally met with countersuits alleging professional incompetence.
- Use carefully worded engagement letters in which the nature and purpose of the engagement are made clear and unmistakable.
- Meet all deadlines.
- Follow all professional standards for auditing.
- Be more selective about new clients. Some potential clients are high risk (i.e., poorly financed, poorly managed, poorly controlled).

Table 8–1   Factors that Enhance Discovery of Computer Theft, Fraud, and Embezzlement

Internal accounting controls
- Separation of duties
- Rotation of duties
- Periodic internal audits and surprise inspections
- Development and documentation of policies, procedures, systems, programs, and program modifications
- Establishment of check signature authorities, dollar authorization limits per signatory, and check total amount limits
- Off-line entry controls and limits

Computer access controls
- Identification defenses
- Authentication defenses
- Establishment of authorizations by levels of authority or levels of security (compartmentalization and "need to know")

Logging of exceptions
- Out of sequence, out of priority, and aborted runs and entries
- Out-of-pattern transactions: too high, too low, too many, too often, too few, unusual file access (odd times and odd places)
- Attempted access beyond authorization level
- Repeated attempts to gain access improperly—wrong password, entry code, and so forth
- Parity and redundancy checks

Variance reporting
- Monitoring operational performance levels for
    - Variations from plans and standards
    - Deviations from accepted or mandated policies, procedures, and practices
    - Deviations from past quantitative relationships (e.g., ratios, proportions, percentages, trends, past performance levels, indices, and so forth)

RESEARCH ON EMBEZZLEMENT

Doing research on the criminologic aspect of embezzlement is a mite boring because most of what has been written is a repetition of the original works of Edwin Sutherland and Donald Cressey. Sutherland (1949) coined the expression "white-collar crime" in his book of the same name, and Cressey (1953) wrote the definitive work on embezzlement entitled *Other People's Money*. The best of the more recent works in the field are Green's *Occupational Crime* (1990), Geis's *On White-Collar Crime* (1982), and *Corporate Crime* by Clinard and Yeager (1980). *The Criminal Elite* by Coleman (1985) is a very useful work too.

If we were to synthesize these works, we might conclude that embezzlers are distinctive in several regards. That is, embezzlers have an unshareable financial problem, generally, as a result of compulsive behaviors such as gambling, substance abuse, and high living; they hold a position of trust that provides easy access to funds or other assets; and they rationalize that converting the funds or assets is not improper because they intend to pay back the owner thereof. Most criminologists tend to agree with that hypothesis as a matter of conventional wisdom. Empirical proof thereof is in short supply, however. Nettler (1982), among others, takes exception to Cressey's method in *Lying, Cheating and Stealing*, citing a Canadian study of six embezzlements in which evidence of an "unshareable financial problem" did not provide a motive—the embezzlers had a variety of motives. Nettler might conclude that, of the three conditions that foster or create an embezzlement situation (motivation, opportunity, and rationalization), motive carries no more weight than opportunity and rationalization.

APPENDIX 8-1

A Selected Chronology of Publicly Reported Embezzlement Incidents, 1982–1992

The following cases of embezzlement are abstracted from various issues of the *Forensic Accounting Review*.[1]

June 1982

Six persons, including four former employees of Banker's Trust Company, were indicted in New York on charges of conspiring to embezzle $1.2 million from the bank. The scheme involved the conversion of funds from inactive accounts that were about to be escheated to New York state. A routine audit uncovered the fraud (*Wall Street Journal*, 5/27/82).

April 1983

A Cleveland, Ohio, United Way accounting supervisor was indicted for embezzling $63,000 from the agency. Checks were issued for specious building and remodeling projects and then endorsed, cashed, or deposited to accounts created for the fictitious contractors (*Cleveland Plain Dealer*, 3/9/83).

A cashier in the Ohio State Treasurer's office pleaded guilty to embezzling $1.15 million. Part of the funds were used to finance the musical ambitions of her boyfriend, a band leader. The cashier had access to public funds in a state vault and could make entries in the state's accounting journals. When cash was counted at the time of audit, the cashier made up shortages by replacing missing funds with fictitious checks (*Cleveland Plain Dealer*, 3/9/83).

July 1983

A former executive of Mr. Coffee (made by North American Systems Inc., of Bedford Heights, Ohio) was indicted for diverting nearly $884,000 of corporate funds to his own use (*Wall Street Journal*, 6/9/83).

---

[1]Jack Bologna. *Forensic Accounting Review*, 1982–1992 issues. Published by Computer Protection Systems, Inc., 150 N. Main, Plymouth, MI 48170.

A former office manager of Walter E. Heller International's Phoenix, Arizona, office was indicted by a state court for diverting $1.9 million. The proceeds were used to acquire real estate holdings (*Wall Street Journal*, 6/8/83).

August 1983

The "big board" charged a cashier of a small brokerage firm with stealing $200,000 of securities from Paine, Webber, Donaldson, and Lufkin. The board also charged twenty other employees of brokerage houses with an assortment of irregularities and fined, suspended temporarily or permanently, a number of such employees (*Wall Street Journal*, 6/28/83).

A court-appointed trustee of a failed Detroit, Michigan, brokerage house was charged with embezzlement by the Securities and Exchange Commission. The trustee, a Detroit attorney, allegedly embezzled over $100,000 and substituted counterfeit bank certificates of deposit to cover the transfer of funds from the trust account to his own personal bank account (*Wall Street Journal*, 7/13/83).

A computer operator employed by the Northampton County, Pennsylvania, Domestic Relations Department was charged with embezzling $84,000. The operator claimed she used the funds to pay for illegal drugs for her boyfriend. She had access to both cash and accounting records and used a "cash lapping" technique to withdraw funds. When apprehended, she demonstrated the technique to her superiors to avoid its occurrence in the future (*Computerworld*, 6/27/83).

November 1983

A former broker with Merrill Lynch pleaded guilty in a New York court to charges she embezzled $174,000 from customer accounts and laundered funds for her wealthy customers (*Wall Street Journal*, 9/30/83).

An employee of Prudential-Bache Securities, Inc., and three confederates were arrested by FBI agents in New York for stealing $5 million in customer dividend checks from the firm (*Wall Street Journal*, 10/12/83).

December 1984

Two EDP employees of Manhattan Industries, Inc., an apparel maker, were recently terminated, and Manhattan then engaged a law firm to investigate whether the two may have been involved in an embezzlement scheme. An attorney for the two former employees called the allegations "groundless and meritless." This is the second time around for Manhattan Industries. It was a victim of a previous embezzlement in 1980. In that case, a credit department director allegedly embezzled $1.5 million. This case involved about $500,000 (*Wall Street Journal*, 11/20/84).

March 1985

A $2.7 million embezzlement charge was made against a freight claims director by his employer, the Chessie System Railroad (*Wall Street Journal*, 2/13/85).

December 1986

David L. Miller, who has admitted embezzling funds from six previous employers but has never been prosecuted, now stands indicted on tax evasion charges for not reporting the embezzled funds (*Wall Street Journal*, 11/20/86).

Robert Richter, a former vice president and controller of Union Labor Life Insurance, pleaded guilty to wire fraud in connection with a $900,000 diversion of the insurance company's funds (*Wall Street Journal*, 12/1/86).

An employee of Detroit's Department of Transportation was charged with authorizing a check for $141,000 to a vendor for work never performed by the vendor (*Crain's Detroit Business*, 11/10/86).

May 1987

Fraud and embezzlement losses at federally insured banks and savings and loans in 1986 were $1.1 billion against losses of $196 million in 1981, reports the FBI. The Justice Department plans to provide more attention to such losses at financial institutions in the future (*Business Week*, 5/18/87).

A stiff seven-and-one-half-year prison sentence was meted out to David L. Miller, a former financial executive who was charged with embezzling $1.3 million from a recent employer. His indictment was his first criminal charge, but he admitted to a *Wall Street Journal* reporter that he had embezzled funds from five previous employers since 1966, none of whom elected to prosecute him after he agreed to pay back the embezzled funds. A psychiatrist testifying in his behalf said he had a "compulsory need to buy love or friendship" (*Wall Street Journal*, 4/29/87).

March 1988

Disneyland may be fun and games for most of us. But its warehouse manager found it more rewarding than his salary. He was accused of masterminding an embezzlement scheme in which he allowed certain toys, souvenirs, and clothing to leave the premises without having been properly billed. The merchandise was then sold to retailers. Some of the merchandise began to show up at flea markets and garage sales at what appeared to be "distress" prices for such new and freshly packaged goods. One curious person called a friend in the security department at Disneyland and bingo! The $500,000 embezzlement was discovered (*Distribution Magazine*, 1/1988).

September 1989

Bank fraud and embezzlement investigations by the FBI soared in 1988 (17,053 in 1988 versus 11,807 investigations in 1987—up 44%). Why the increase? Perhaps because of bank and savings and loan failures (*Security Letter*, 7/17/89).

Embezzlement of more than $1 million was alleged against a former branch manager at Society for Savings Bankroll in Hartford, Connecticut. The embezzlement was discovered during a routine internal audit. The FBI is investigating the matter, but formal criminal charges have not been brought yet (*Wall Street Journal*, 8/11/89).

October 1989

A former Housing and Urban Development (HUD) accountant is indicted for allegedly embezzling $1 million from a federal program intended to help the poor acquire housing (*Wall Street Journal*, 8/30/89).

Fraud is booming at banks. Why? Tony Adamski, the FBI's chief of financial crimes, says that before 1982, most bank losses were from teller embezzlements. Now it goes to the top. Bank, savings and loans, and credit union fraud and embezzlement losses rose from $382.3 million in 1983 to $2.19 billion in 1988 (*Detroit Free Press*, 9/15/89).

March 1990

A veteran city employee in Ann Arbor, Michigan, stands accused of embezzling $92,000. The employee, a clerk in the transportation department, submitted phony invoices for road patch material, salt, sand, gravel, and hot asphalt using the pretense that the goods were supplied by a subcontractor of a firm with whom the city had a legitimate contract. When the first of the set of checks was issued, the clerk attempted to cash it at a nearby bank. Without an assumed name on file, the bank would not honor the check. The clerk filed an assumed name and opened a new account at the bank. The bank then honored the checks, but she was tripped up when another clerk, in reconciling canceled checks, noticed that the transportation clerk's name appeared on a check as the second endorser (*Ann Arbor News*, 2/27/90).

In another Michigan city embezzlement, the city clerk of Imlay City skimmed $226,000 from residents' tax and utility bills. She knew the system's internal control weaknesses because she had supervised the installation of a new computer billing application. She was the only employee who understood the system (*Detroit Free Press*, 2/7/90).

July 1990

A young bank officer in Kuala Lumpur, Malaysia, compromised the computer's security system and stole $1.5 million. He drew heat to himself when he bought a Lamborghini, three Porsches, and a Mercedes (*Ann Arbor News*, 6/18/90).

April 1991

A thirty-year, veteran employee of Manufacturers National Bank of Detroit pleaded guilty to embezzling $1.2 million over a ten-year period. The embezzled funds were used to pay for cars, gambling, jewelry, and a home swimming pool (*Detroit Free Press*, 1/29/91).

The former CEO of a Nebraska credit union that failed pleaded guilty to embezzlement charges. The credit union's failure was the second largest in history (*Wall Street Journal*, 2/12/91).

May 1992

A bank lending officer at the People's Bank of Hamtramck, Michigan, pleaded guilty to stealing $8 million from the bank over a three-year period. The "MO" was typical for a lending officer. He created 599 fake loans. As loans came due, he created new loans to pay off the old ones. Some of the stolen money was used to pay gambling debts in Atlantic City and Las Vegas. He kept $416,000 in cash in the trunk of his car. Police also found $40,000 in an Arkansas state park and $50,000 in a local safe deposit box. This is untypical of embezzlers who usually blow it all on "wine, women (or men), and song" (*Detroit Free Press*, 4/11/92).

An accountant for Detroit's public schools stands accused of embezzling $1.3 million over a five-year period by issuing 145 checks for nonexistent goods and services. He was apprehended at a bank branch while attempting to cash a $48,999 check drawn on the school system's imprest cash fund. He was controller of the fund (*Detroit Free Press*, 3/24/92).

Detroit was not alone in surfacing embezzlements last month. A Newark, New Jersey, bank was victimized by one of its employees too—to the tune of $2.4 million over four years. The defendant transferred funds from his employer bank to four other local banks, to accounts he controlled. To conceal his activities, he enlisted an employee of a stock brokerage firm who transferred funds from the broker's accounts to the bank (*Wall Street Journal*, 4/29/92).

An alleged embezzlement by a former chief financial officer at Marietta Corp. forced it to revise financial statements for the 1987 through 1990 years. The revisions resulted in a decrease in profit of about $1.5 million over the three-year period (*Wall Street Journal*, 3/19/92).

A former executive vice-president of Service Merchandise, Inc., is alleged to have embezzled $850,000 by using false, forged, or altered invoices (*Nashville Tennessean*, 4/9/92).

9

Corporate and Financial Fraud

Management by objectives (MBO) is a concept long heralded in management literature for its utility and versatility in planning, directing, and controlling large organizations. The MBO concept suggests that a formalized goal-setting and monitoring process is the surest way of achieving better individual performance and better corporate results. In essence, MBO is part of the strategic- and profit-planning process. Corporate goals are defined in terms of expected rates of return on investment for each profit center of a company. These dollarized expectations are then translated into forecasts of revenue, expenses, and profits.

As any second-year student of accounting knows, profit can be "juggled" by various methods, such as failing to properly record expenses, recording sales that are not yet finalized, and overstating inventory. In fact, these are the favorite techniques of profit-center managers hell-bent on making their budgets come true in feast-or-famine times. The other technique is to provide a little "water" in the budget forecast document by either understating expected revenue or overstating expenses and capital needs, or both. The budget

71

review process, however, is designed to thwart the latter sort of financial trickery. Budget reviews are supposed to keep the game players honest. The give-and-take of budget reviews generally ends with some sort of compromise between boss and subordinate on expectations for revenue, costs, profits, and capital expenditures.

In hard times, bosses tend to bargain harder and compromise less, if at all. In good times, bosses generally split the difference or at least are more generous in the terms they impose on subordinates. So the strategy that smart subordinates use to win in these annual contests changes with the times. In good times, revenue is under-estimated and expenses are overestimated. In poor times, the strategy is reversed. Ergo, the main problem with budgets is that neither bosses nor subordinates have any imperative to deal with the data contained in them from a reality perspective.

The MBO concept, however, promotes the notion that reality lies within a range. Nothing in life is perfect or absolute so why pretend it is different in a budget? Budgets, say the MBO experts like Dr. George S. Odiorne, should be stated in terms of pessimistic (worse case) scenario, a realistic scenario, and an optimistic scenario (best case). That way, all the game playing can be avoided during the budget review process. And, with upper and lower limits on the revenue and expense numbers, management by exception can be practiced. When numbers fall below the pessimistic scenario, an immediate report and explanation of the condition is issued by the subordinate to his or her superior. "I'm in trouble," he or she says in essence. "I may need some help from you. I may even have to revise the rest of my forecast downward."

But that sort of honesty and candor does not exist in many of the firms who claim to be managing by objectives. In fact, financial goals are stated in terms of a single-column array. Goals are not stated in terms of pessimistic, realistic, or optimistic expectations— not even in terms of a one-column bank of numbers with a permissible plus-and-minus variance factor. So, all variances are reportable "violations" of the budget, which makes for a mountain of explanations for trivialities. Ultimately, such a system of management by trivialities tends to corrupt all the actors. We have seen evidence of such corruption in a spate of Securities and Exchange Commission (SEC) actions against major companies whose profit-center managers "fudged" their operating data to hide losses or reported false numbers because it was what their bosses wanted to hear or even to enhance their own bonus awards.

Both the profit-center manager and his or her superior at corporate headquarters have a financial stake in the unit's profitability. Success may bring on a glow of personal pride in its achievement, but it usually also means a fatter paycheck—for both employees. So, there is a dual temptation to cheat a little—the superior for not looking too deeply into the subordinate's report numbers and the subordinate for "juggling" the numbers to make them come out right.

THE AUDITOR AS REALITY THERAPIST

Into this fray comes the auditor—the person who has no axe to grind or ox to gore. The auditor deals in reality therapy. He or she sees things as they are—or certainly should—because his or her job requires it. The auditor has the unenviable job of keeping everyone reasonably honest, even his or her own management superiors. That's a real challenge today. Auditors want promotions too, and pay raises and prestige as well. But fortunately they do not seem to be as ready to compromise their principles to achieve those goals as a few line managers. Admittedly, the number of conniving executives is relatively small. The damage they do to the image of managers in general is, however, quite substantial. So, how much conniving should we accept from profit-center managers and their headquarters' superiors? The SEC does not seem to be inclined to accept much conniving today. If auditors ever needed a mandate to ferret out executive fraud of the financial type, they have it now.

But ferreting out financial reporting frauds is not as simple as it sounds. The players are a rather sophisticated lot and often know as much about the accounting rules as do the auditors. Although internal controls are designed to keep the game honest, internal controls can be bypassed or overridden by higher authorities. Controls are designed to keep honest people honest. Dishonest people are not often discouraged or thwarted by even the best controls. And, in an environment in which executive compensation is based on short-term results, both senior management and middle management have an economic incentive to play fast and loose with operating data.

RED FLAGS OF FRAUD IN CORPORATIONS

Table 9–1 lists a few things you might wish to add to your repertoire in an audit where there is a reasonable concern about the honesty of management, the integrity of data, or the adequacy of controls. These are not proofs of fraud; they are simply "red flags" that might cause you to enlarge the scope of your audit. Any one (1) "yes" answer may be a symptom of "game playing" with profits, outright fraud, or embezzlement. On the other hand, fifteen (15) or more "yes" answers is a very strong indication that this is no ordinary audit.

Table 9–1   Fraud "Red Flags"

- Is the company in a highly competitive industry known for its predatory practices?
- Does high turnover exist at the senior management level?
- Are outside auditors changed frequently?
- Are there persistent cash flow shortages?
- Is the demand for the company's products or services waning?
- Is the quality of operational and financial planning poor?
- Is morale low?
- Are employees abused, exploited, or underpaid?
- Is top management low-trust and autocratic?
- Does the company engage in unethical competitive practices?
- Is there much mistrust between management and nonmanagement people?
- Is there evidence of interpersonal hostility at senior management levels?
- Is the company in a continuous battle with government regulators and taxing authorities?
- Are there frequent overrides of controls by senior management?
- Do the records show evidence of many off-line transactions?
- Do the off-line transactions involve the moving of cash?
- Do the same people always approve or process off-line transactions?
- Are there any credible allegations that senior managers are engaged in fraudulent or illegal activities?
- Is there any evidence of inventory overstatement, fictitious sales, nonexistent employees on the payroll, or overpayments to vendors?
- Is there any evidence of year-end adjusting of journal entries that appear questionable?
- Is there any evidence of lapping on accounts receivable, check kiting, early booking of sales, or expense deferrals?

RED FLAGS OF FRAUD IN FINANCIAL INSTITUTIONS

Certain common elements are often present in serious cases of insider and outsider abuse in financial institutions, giving rise to unsafe or unsound practices or other violations of the federal (and often state) banking statutes. What follows are some examples of "abuse flags" utilized by both the Federal Deposit Insurance Corporation (FDIC) and the Federal Home Loan Bank Board (FHLBB) during the examination process:

> (a) a change in control followed by a dramatic change in operational philosophy; (b) large influx of brokered savings; (c) large loan concentrations by borrower; indications of "straw borrowers" (nominees); (d) large loan (or investment) concentrations by area; (e) a sudden high degree of speculative lending; (f) excessive loans to one borrower; (g) large loans (or investments) funding quickly with poor documentation; (h) questionable appraisals supporting large loans; (i) large amount of non-cash income, excessive loan fees, accrued interest, interest reserves, etc.; (j) large increase in scheduled items; (k) large loans refinanced when due; (l) unusual compensation, fees, bonuses, or fringe benefits paid to insiders; (m) obvious (or apparent) relationships between borrowers and insiders; (n) insiders apparently benefiting (directly or indirectly) from loans granted; and (o) highly unusual transactions in which management's explanation makes little, if any, economic sense.

The FBI has described the most prevalent types or patterns of criminal misconduct; based on its experience, large dollar losses from fraud or embezzlement, which often lead to failures of financial institutions, result from commercial or real estate loan transactions which usually involve insider participation. The five most common types of schemes utilized against financial institutions are as follows:

1. *Nominee Loans*—Loans obtained by one person on behalf of an undisclosed person. The nominee or "straw borrower" typically has no involvement in the loan transaction other than to pose as the borrower.

2. *Double Pledging of Collateral*—Loans obtained at two or more different financial institutions by pledging the same property as collateral. The combined amount of the loans exceeds the value of the property and the borrower does not disclose the pledging of the property as collateral to a previous loan.

3. *Reciprocal Loan Arrangements*—Loans made to insiders of a financial institution or sold to the financial institution itself based on an agreement with insiders of another financial institution to reciprocate in future loan transactions. This arrangement results in less-than-arms-length transactions between insiders of the two financial institutions and has been used previously to conceal loans from [federal agency] examiners.

4. *Land Flip*—Transfers of land between related parties to fraudulently inflate the value of the land. The land is used as collateral for loans based on the inflated or fraudulent valuation. Loan amounts typically greatly exceed the actual value of the land.

5. *Linked Financing*—The practice of depositing money into a financial institution with the understanding that the financial institution will make a loan conditioned on receipt of the deposits.

10

The Evolution of a Corporate Fraud

Last year was a banner year for ABCO Co., a consumer product manufacturer that is number two in its industry. Revenue, profit, and marketshare reached record levels. This year's financial plan calls for a modest increase of 10% in revenue, 8% in gross profit, and an increase in marketshare of one half of 1%, to be taken mainly from its number one competitor, XYZ Co. If these goals are reached, there is a bonus kicker for everyone. ABCO Co.'s Midwest division shared in the good fortune of its parent company last year and this year optimistically forecasted revenue, gross profit, and marketshare increases in accordance with the corporatewide plan.

Midwest division came through the first quarter with flying colors—right on target. But in month four of this year, consumers, as they are wont to do in this industry, spent their money on other things. Sales, profit, and marketshare goals were not reached. That was hard to swallow at headquarters, but the problem was national. So the Midwest division was forgiven for its transgression but admonished to move more decisively to correct the problem.

Unfortunately, in month five, sales slumped again for both ABCO's Midwest division and XYZ's Midwest division. But XYZ Co. countered with a heavy advertising and price-slashing strategy to move its products in the marketplace. This caught ABCO Co.'s Midwest division off guard. When sales, profits, and marketshare were reported by ABCO's Midwest division to headquarters, the feedback was crude and the implications were not so subtle: "Get your numbers to come out right or we'll get somebody who can."

The Midwest general manager and his regional director of sales called a meeting of all sales personnel and made it clear that customers had to be "worked over" with a heavy hand and "loaded down" with products. The goals had to be met. Without additional advertising and price cuts, retailers and consumers were not about to take any more of ABCO's product. As month six was coming to an end and disaster loomed on the horizon, the sales manager ordered the salesmen handling the biggest accounts to process fictitious sales through the accounting system to "buy some time." The fictitious sales could be reversed by credit memos in the month following. The salesmen did as they were told but showed some concern about inventory levels giving away their little scheme. "We will take care of that next month if we have to," said the sales manager.

Month seven came and sales again were soft. The sales manager then had to enlist the aid of the production and warehouse managers, whom he asked to "juggle the inventory for a month," as a favor. But month eight came and went and actual sales were still off. Inflated sales by that time came to $5 million and now all customer accounts were being manipulated at month end and relieved by credit memos during the month following. By year end, everyone in sales, accounting, data processing, production, and warehousing was involved in the scheme, which, by then, involved a sales overstatement of $10 million.

ABCO's total sales are $500 million this year. You are the audit manager of the public accounting firm that does the audit of ABCO's Midwest division. What would you do: (1) if the above information were brought to your attention before you commenced your audit?, (2) you learned about it from an employee during your audit?, or (3) you found the errors and irregularities in the sales and inventory accounts during your audit?

X-CORP.—CREDIT UNION CASE

Scenario

X-Corp. is a U.S. multinational computer manufacturer. The company has enlightened policies with respect to its human resources. It provides generous salaries and benefits and rarely lays off employees. It subscribes to a fair employment practices code and is highly regarded by the mass media for its sense of social responsibility. An incidental benefit it provides its employees is a federally chartered credit union. Historically, the general manager has come from the ranks of the company's middle management or finance staff. The current incumbent is the former manager of corporate administrative services.

The X-Corp. federal credit union has fallen on bad times since government deregulation of financial institutions in 1978. Profits have been sagging because of large loan losses, the high cost of funds, high G&A expenses, and a staff relatively unskilled in the new technologies of banking and finance (e.g., CDs, money market accounts, credit cards, home equity mortgages, commercial loans, construction loans, stock and bond trading, futures trading in commodities and currencies, investments in jumbo CDs, reverse repos, computerized recordkeeping, electronic funds transfers, and so on).

This year the credit union's general manager found it necessary to terminate the chief financial officer (CFO), a thirty-year veteran of X-Corp. The man was unable to cope with all the changes in banking laws and technology. The departure was amicable, however. The former CFO was given a generous early retirement bonus after executing a waiver of rights to sue for discriminatory employment practices. He is now basking in the sun in the Cayman Islands.

Because of your knowledge and experience in matters of accounting, finance, law, investigation, and criminology, you were hired to replace him at his annual salary of $50,000, plus a bonus, if profits are improved. During your first month on the job, you discover the items in the following list. Questions appear after the various events to guide you in dealing with the situations.

1. The accounting records are a mess.
2. There are irreconcilable differences in the general ledger, to the tune of $500,000.

3. Entries with respect to investments are not made contemporaneously with transactions; some entries are made months after the transactions.

QUESTION 1: What legal, audit, or investigative action would you take?

4. The broker through whom jumbo CDs are purchased and sold has not supplied transaction documents for all transactions and has failed to provide an accounting or confirmation of balances even after repeated requests by the outside auditor.

5. Some of the jumbo CDs bought and sold by the credit union were of failed savings and loans. Although these investments are protected up to $100,000 each, some of the CDs were of larger denominations. We do not know the current status of these CDs.

6. The former CFO was alleged to have been trading in stocks, bonds, commodities, and futures (or all of them) on his own account with the same broker.

QUESTION 2: What legal, audit, or investigative action would you take now?

7. On a few occasions, the former CFO had used a company credit card for personal expenses (i.e., family vacation). When questioned, he admitted the same orally and in writing, and made partial restitution. The balance was repaid to the credit union by its fidelity bond carrier. The loss claim was less than $2,000.

QUESTION 3: What legal, audit, or investigative action would you take?

8. The CFO used a PC with spreadsheet software to keep track of the credit union's investments in jumbo CDs and for certain other accounting applications. The data was encrypted, however, and, thus far, no one has been able to break the code.

QUESTION 4: What legal, audit, or investigative action would you take now?

9. A review of the former CFO's share draft (checking) account at the credit union shows he frequented a bar and made monthly payments on a condominium owned by a woman who worked for him as a data-entry clerk.

QUESTION 5: What legal, audit, or investigative action would you take now?

10. A review of the CFO's credit card transactions shows he purchased a $3,000 diamond ring while in Las Vegas last year.

QUESTION 6: What legal, audit, or investigative action would you take now?

11. An anonymous source writes to you and says the former CFO has a secret bank account in the Caymans and just paid $200,000 in cash for a condominium. He is also about to divorce his wife. The CFO made these comments to the source in a barroom conversation.

QUESTION 7: What legal, audit, or investigative action would you take?

12. A confidential source of known reliability tells you the former CFO lost $100,000 to a reputed Mafia bookmaker last year. He welshed on the bet and is now being sought by a well-known hitman of the mob.

QUESTION 8: What legal, audit, or investigative action would take now?

13. The audit staff of the federal regulatory agency for credit unions, after a few days on site, advises you that loan and operating losses and the mysterious disappearance of assets will eat up your statutory reserves and make you insolvent unless you can prove to their satisfaction that a bond claim for honesty and faithful performance will be presented immediately to the insurance carrier and that said claim has some reasonable chance of being paid.

QUESTION 9: What legal, audit, or investigative action would you take now?

QUESTION 10: Summarize the facts and issues of the case and prepare a memo to the U.S. attorney.

The appendix that follows will be useful to any auditor who needs to investigate corporate fraud.

APPENDIX 10-1

The Corporate Fraud Auditor's Checklist

Company Culture—Is top management:

- Focused on short-term profits?
- Autocratic?
- Low-trust?
- Noncommunicative?
- Poor in planning?
- Devoid of ethics?
- Insensitive to stakeholders (customers, stockholders, employees)?
- Motivated only by economic rewards?
- Deficient in vision?
- Deficient in establishing controls?
- Deficient in monitoring controls?
- Corrupt?
- Incompetent?
- Given to creating stress for lower-level management?
- Given to high turnover?
- Given to frequent changing of external auditors and outside counsel?

Control History—Is there evidence of:

- Past history of regulatory noncompliance?
- Persistent cash flow shortages?
- Predatory practices in the industry?
- Price-fixing in the industry?
- Corruptive practices in the industry?
- Weak or absent internal controls?
- Loosely enforced internal controls?
- Internal corruption problems?
- Pending litigation instituted by shareholders, lenders, or regulators?
- Diminishing cash flow and/or sales and income?
- Increasing inventory, payables, receivables, and/or cost of sales?
- Decreasing freight-in and/or freight-out charges?
- Increasing receivables write-offs?
- Increasing reclassifications of income and expense items?
- Increasing year-end adjustments?
- Booking sales that are not really finalized?
- Delaying necessary repairs and maintenance?
- Not making adequate provision for doubtful accounts receivable?
- Capitalizing expenses that should have been charged to the current year?
- Related party transactions?
- Overstatement of revenue, assets, and/or earnings?
- Understatement of expenses, liabilities, and/or losses?
- Destruction or alteration of records?
- "Smoothing" of profits?

11

Celebrated Cases of Corporate Accounting Improprieties

Among the landmark cases of accounting improprieties are two cases that literally shook the audit community out of its lethargy: *McKesson and Robbins* and *Equity Funding*. McKesson's impropriety was overstating its inventory; indeed, claiming inventory that did not even exist. This case led to a change in audit requirements of public companies that added an inventory count to audit procedures. *Equity Funding* is celebrated as one of the largest accounting frauds in audit history in terms of amount of overstated revenue ($200 million), number of conspirators (several hundred accounting, finance, data processing, internal audit, and high-level executives), along with a contingent of external auditors.

The *Equity Funding* case began in 1966 with a simple overstatement of assets. Earnings continued to be inflated each year thereafter. By the time the case became a matter of public knowledge in 1973, the fraud had taken on gigantic proportions, as summarized here:

- Assets had been overstated by more than $100 million.
- Fictitiously funded loans to policyholders totaled $62.3 million.
- Fictitious commercial paper totaled $8 million.
- In 1972, Equity Funding listed assets of $737.5 million and a net worth of $143.4 million. The subsequent investigation and audit showed actual assets to be worth $488.9 million and actual net worth to be a negative $42 million.
- More than 200 insiders were aware of some aspect of the fraud before its exposure.
- Thousands of fictitious insurance policies were generated by company computers.
- Stock certificates were counterfeited in the company's print shop.
- Before the dust settled, twenty-two former company officers and three auditors were indicted on mail fraud, stock fraud, filing false financial statements, interstate transportation of counterfeit securities, and illegal wiretapping charges.

Let us look at a few other celebrated corporate accounting improprieties to see if there are any common threads. We begin with a landmark case: *H. J. Heinz*. As you may know, Heinz has been a household name for quality food products for about a hundred years. The company has been well managed, profitable, and socially responsible; but in the late 1970s, it received much unfavorable publicity for what appeared to be a minor financial flaw. Some of its profit-center managers engaged in accounting irregularities of the kind most people do not understand. They understated sales, overstated some expenses, and deferred other expenses to the next year, thereby reducing their unit's profits. Profits were reduced to create a "cushion" for the next year. If business was bad, they could dip into their slush funds and pull out enough profit to meet the goals negotiated with company headquarters. The total amount of these profit obfuscations was quite small ($8.5 million) compared to overall sales ($2.4 billion). It was just that actual sales and profits were not as reported to the Internal Revenue Service, the Securities and Exchange Commission (SEC), and their stockholders.

Because the corporation is highly decentralized, headquarter's people claimed they were unaware of the lower level "hanky-panky." Headquarters monitored them through budget forecasts of sales and expenses and an incentive compensation plan that paid off better if you met the high end of your profit goals. The other watchword was consistent growth in profits. Top management was committed to that overriding goal, and indeed the company's earnings did consistently rise (1978 marked the fifteenth consecutive year of record profits).

The company had an explicit policy that prohibited its divisions from having any form of unrecorded assets or false entries in its books and records—and Heinz did not measure short-term performance alone. The top nineteen officials, including division general managers, had a long-term incentive plan in addition to the one-year plan.

In a nutshell, initially what there was was income transferral aided and abetted by vendors who supplied invoices one year for services not rendered until the next year. When that was not enough, false invoices were submitted one year and then reversed in the following year. The amounts involved did not have a material effect on the company's reported profits.

What can we learn from this case? For one thing, exerting pressure for continuous growth in profits may well foster improper accounting practices, particularly if coupled with an incentive compensation plan that rewards and reinforces continuous growth on the high side. For another thing, autonomous units with independent accounting capabilities may be tempted, under these circumstances, to manipulate performance data. For example, the following practices evolved at one Heinz division:

- Year-end shipments were delayed to justify invoicing them in the following year.
- When some customers complained about the delays, the shipments were made, but shipping and invoice documents were misdated.
- Credits from vendors were not recorded until the following year.
- "Income management" became a way of life. One employee was given the task of maintaining private records to ensure the recovery of amounts paid to vendors on improper invoices.
- The practice of delayed shipment and prepaid billing permeated the division down to the departmental level to ensure that departmental budgeted amounts were met.
- Ten separate vendors joined in supplying improper invoices.

- Other questionable tactics to manipulate income included inflated accruals, inventory adjustments, commodity transactions, and fictitious customer rebates.

Heinz, however, is not the only case in which autonomous accounting and/or pressure for performance led to manipulations of records. Similar episodes occurred at Datapoint Corp., Saxon Industries, Ronson Corp., Pepsico, AM International, U.S. Surgical, Stauffer Chemical, and McCormick and Co. The following briefly describes what happened at these companies:

Datapoint Corp., a San Antonio computer manufacturer, was the subject of a stockholder's suit that claimed the firm misrepresented its financial data by engaging in a "warehousing and brokerage scheme" to inflate sales. Customer orders were booked in advance as sales by some of Datapoint's marketing representatives to achieve sales goals. This later resulted in an unusually high level of returned products, according to the firm's chief executive officer (*MIS Week*, 8/18/82).

Saxon Industries, Inc., and three former executives were cited by the SEC for falsifying company records. The SEC charged that the officials created fictional inventories of $75 million by listing additional inventory after the physical count was completed, by programming the company's computers to automatically add inventory, and by transferring fake inventories from one division to another (*Wall Street Journal*, 9/10/82).

The SEC, in an administrative proceeding, took action against Ronson Corp. concerning the accounting practices followed by a former Ronson subsidiary in California (Ronson Hydraulic Units Corporation—Rhucor). For a five-year period prior to 1980, Rhucor understated its expenses and recorded sales for products that had not been shipped. These tactics resulted in an overstatement of profits by the subsidiary that was allegedly committed to meet the unit's profit goals. Arbitrary increases were also allegedly made to the unit's monthly ending inventory to overstate profits for the period. Ronson settled the charges with the SEC by neither admitting nor denying them, and agreeing to report accurately in the future (*Wall Street Journal*, 11/8/82).

Pepsico, Inc., was sued by two shareholders who alleged it filed false and misleading financial statements because of irregularities in its overseas operations. The irregularities resulted in $92.1 million in overstated earnings over a five-year period and overstated assets of $79.4 million. Pepsico itself made the irregularities known after it conducted its own investigation into the matter. Internal controls have since been tightened and a dozen employees of its foreign subsidiary have been terminated (*Wall Street Journal*, 12/20/82).

AM International was charged by the SEC with illegally inflating its profits by $23 million in its 1980 and 1981 fiscal years. The Commission charged AM International recorded as "sold," products being rented by customers and products that had not been shipped. Inventory overstatements were also reported (*Wall Street Journal*, 5/3/83).

In a lawsuit, the SEC charged that U.S. Surgical Corp. overstated its pretax earnings from 1979 through 1981 by at least $18.4 million through accounting irregularities that included falsified purchase orders; unordered products shipped to hospitals and carried on the books as sales; and consignments of goods to European distributors, which were listed as sales. Some $4 million in legal costs were also spread over several years rather than being accounted for in the year or years they were incurred. As part of the settlement of the charges, the firm's president was required to repay $317,000 in bonuses he had previously received (*Wall Street Journal*, 2/28/84).

In a "first-of-a-kind" case, the SEC charged a supplier firm with aiding a customer company to violate federal securities laws. In a civil suit, the SEC charged that Barden Co., a Danbury, Connecticut, supplier of surgical equipment, assisted the U.S. Surgical Corp. of Norwalk, Connecticut, by providing it with false invoices, allowing it to capitalize costs that should have been expensed. A Barden vice president also confirmed to U.S. Surgical's auditors that the false invoices were correct. Barden consented to a court order barring them from further violations of the securities laws (*Wall Street Journal*, 6/27/84).

Stauffer Chemical Co. of Westport, Connecticut, was sued by the SEC in a civil action alleging Stauffer overstated its 1982 earnings by $31.1 million. According to the SEC, Stauffer effected consignments of some agricultural chemicals to its dealers and reported the consignments as sales in 1982 rather than sales in 1983. Earnings were therefore understated for 1983 but overstated for 1982, the SEC said. Stauffer settled the suit without admitting or denying the SEC charges (*Wall Street Journal*, 8/14/84).

Expanding further, this quote is from *Fraud Auditing and Forensic Accounting* (Bologna, 1987):

> In the *McCormick* case, the SEC's complaint alleged that McCormick inflated reported current earnings by deferring recognition of various expenses and by increasing reported revenues by accounting for goods ready for shipment as current sales, even though they were not shipped until a later period. These irregularities occurred in autonomous divisions and involved a number of employees in middle-management roles. These employees believed the improper practices were the only way to achieve the profit goals set arbitrarily by a distant, centralized corporate management. Several employees stated they viewed their activities as a team effort, all for the benefit of the company. There was no evidence that corporate funds were diverted for the personal benefit of any McCormick employee (p. 44).

In *AM International*, the Commission alleged that AMI grossly overstated its results of operations, assets, and shareholder's equity, understated liabilities, and misstated statements of changes in financial position. How did AMI accomplish this?

Inventory losses were deferred and ending inventory overstated; books were kept open after cutoff dates to increase reported sales and earnings; sales were recorded although products were not shipped; sales were inflated by deliberate double-billing; operating leases were recorded as sales; allowances for losses were recorded although the products were shipped only to branch offices and a public warehouse, not to customers; accounting policies were changed to increase earnings without disclosure of the changes in policy; known errors that caused increased earnings were ignored; intercompany accounts were out of balance and the differences arbitrarily reclassified as inventories; known inaccuracies in books and records were not investigated, let alone resolved; costs of sales were manipulated, and accounts payable were simply not recorded.

The organizational environment aired in the AMI complaint made a highly negative impression on the Commission. Two excerpts from the SEC complaint exemplify this environment:

> During the course of the 1980 fiscal year, AM International's financial position deteriorated and its management then applied increas-

ing pressure on the divisions to meet performance goals. Such pressure consisted of, among other means, threatened dismissals, actual dismissals, and character attacks on certain of the division's senior management. This pressure was in turn applied by the division's senior management to middle management. These pressures were motivated in part by the desire of AMI to have a public offering of its securities in the fall of 1980, and the belief that a pretax profit of $10 to $12 million for the 1980 fiscal year was necessary in order to proceed with the offering. . . .

In response to the pressure . . . various divisions . . . engaged in widespread and pervasive accounting irregularities . . . in order to present results of operations which conformed to budget performance objectives. Throughout the 1980 fiscal year, AMI's corporate headquarters learned of many instances of accounting irregularities employed by its divisions. Despite this knowledge, AMI continued to pressure its divisions to meet projected operating results (Bologna, 1987, pp. 44–45).

As Bologna (1987) states, the Commission's complaint in *U.S. Surgical* alleged that Surgical:

1. Issued falsified purchase orders to vendors who in turn submitted untrue invoices so that Surgical's reported cost of parts was decreased and its reported costs of materials was improperly capitalized by over $4 million.
2. Shipped significant quantities of unordered products to customers and recorded them as sales.
3. Improperly treated shipments on consignments to its dealers, salespeople, and certain foreign entities as sales, resulting in cumulative overstatement of income by over $2 million.
4. Improperly failed to write off assets that could not be located or had been scrapped, and capitalized certain operating costs as overhead, increasing earnings by millions of dollars.
5. Improperly capitalized approximately $4 million of legal costs, purportedly for the defense of certain patents, when those costs did not relate to the defense of patents but were recurring operating expenses (pp. 45–46).

Table 11–1 contains a more complete list of celebrated cases of accounting improprieties. The following are some environmental causes of accounting improprieties:

Table 11–1   Accounting Impropriety Cases

American International	North American Acceptance
American Biomaterials Corp.	OPM Leasing
Cenco, Inc.	Penn Square Bank
Coated Sales	Pepsico
Crazy Eddie	PharMor
Datapoint	Regina Vacuum Cleaners
Equity Funding	Rocky Mount Undergarment Co.
ESM Government Securities	Sahlen Associates
Four Seasons Nursing Homes	Saxon Industries
Gucci American, Inc.	Stauffer Chemical
H. J. Heinz	Stirling Homex
Leslie Fay	J. Walter Thompson
Mattel, Inc	U.S. Financial
McCormick Spices	U.S. Surgical
Miniscribe	ZZZZ Best

- Pressure for performance
- Industry competition
- Industry mores
- Reward system
- Organizational structure
- Goal-setting process
- Quality and integrity of management
- Control system
- Code of ethics
- Quality of auditing

These are common corporate accounting improprieties:

- Overstated inventory
- Unrecorded liabilities
- Diverted cash
- Fabricated revenue
- Anticipated revenue
- Revenue transferral
- Expense deferral
- Fabricated expenses
- Disguised payments

Lest we forget, there were also celebrated accounting impropri-eties cases in "regulated" industries such as banking, brokerage, and defense contracting (e.g., Penn Square Bank, United American Bank, Drysdale Securities, ESM Government Securities, Bevil Bressler, sav-ings and loans (too numerous to list all of them), Teledyne, Grum-man, Sundstrand, ITT, General Electric, Unisys, Boeing, General Dynamics, Rockwell, Lockheed, and so on). **Note**, however, that most of these incidents occurred some time ago and are not a reflec-tion on these companies' current management.

12

Investigating Crimes For and Against the Corporation

Criminal acts can be directed against a corporation by insiders as well as outsiders. Insiders include directors, officers, employees, and agents. Outsiders include vendors, suppliers, contractors, customers, competitors, and underworld elements.

Crimes directed against a corporation by outsiders are generally intended to cause loss of or damage to assets of the company. Crimes by corporate insiders, on the other hand, can either be intended to enhance the economic performance of the company or to cause loss of or damage to assets; so, crimes by corporate insiders can be intended to be both for and against the best economic interests of a company.

We might, therefore, say that corporate crime is crime committed by insiders, for or against the economic interests of their company, and by outsiders whose intentions are to cause damage to the company. Fraud (deception) plays a central role in most corporate crimes by insiders and outsiders. Fraudulent acts can be either detected or proven by the use of auditing techniques because, at some point in the commission of fraud, cash or other assets are transferred, converted, diverted, or overstated; liabilities are understated; and income is either overstated or understated. In any event, corporate crimes usually have an impact on corporate books of account, records, documents, and financial statements.

Crimes committed for the corporation might include violations of laws or regulations promulgated and enforced by federal agencies such as the FBI, IRS, FTC, OSHA, FDA, SEC, EPA, National Highway Transportation Safety Board (NHTSB), the Consumer Protection Agency, and the Anti-Trust Division of the Department of Justice. Crimes committed against a corporation might include theft or destruction of assets, embezzlement of funds, and corruption by vendors or contractors. As you can see, in crimes for the corporation, the entity is, in a sense, a perpetrator. (If caught however, it becomes a victim in the sense of having to pay legal fees, fines, penalties, and/or damages for the illegal acts of its agents.)

On the other hand, a corporation may be a pure victim in crimes (e.g., fraud, theft, embezzlement, etc.) committed against it by its own directors, officers, employees, and agents. But a corporation may become a victim of crimes committed by outsiders as well as insiders. For example, a corporation may become a victim of a crime committed against it by a supplier (e.g., corruption of a purchasing department official, defrauding the corporation by substituting an inferior quality of merchandise or raw material than ordered, or double-billing for the same order). A competitor may corrupt an employee to secure proprietary information. An underworld figure may extort funds to guarantee labor peace. A political authority may seek a bribe to get a government agency to act favorably toward the economic interests of the company or to compromise a political official about to impose a penalty on the company.

HOW EXTENSIVE IS CORPORATE CRIME?

Just how pervasive is corporate crime? And how likely is it to be discovered? Corporate crime may not be large in number of incidents but its social and economic impacts are often felt around the world of finance. Fraud alone now involves big numbers and big companies. Within the past fifteen or so years, we have seen corporate frauds in which losses to the corporations themselves and to their shareholders exceeded $200 million. Celebrated cases include

Equity Funding, Volkswagen AG, ESM Government Securities, Drysdale Securities, and OPM Leasing.

A few years ago, *Fortune* magazine noted a study it did of the top 1,000 industrial corporations and indicated that over a period of about ten years, 11% of those firms were charged with some form of corporate crime (e.g., commercial and political bribery, antitrust violations, tax and securities violations). These were mainly in the category of fraud for the company. If we add frauds committed against those companies by their employees, vendors, and customers, the percentage of those *Fortune* 1,000 companies, which may have experienced frauds, would seemingly be higher, perhaps even double the 11% mentioned before. Frauds of the type we are speaking of here (corporate frauds—for and against the company) can involve very large sums of money. So, although the incidence rate may be relatively low, the potential dollar loss may be correspondingly very high.

A book on corporate crime should perhaps contain some reference to the current situation; that is, whether corporate crime is rising, stable, decreasing, or changing its character. In all truth, we must say that hard data on that subject is difficult to find. Educated guesses are what we have found. If we were to make an educated guess, we would say corporate crime is rising both in incidents and average amount of loss.

Until the 1970s, $100 million corporate frauds were rare, but the Equity Funding case changed that. The case involved a $200 million overstatement of insurance sales and a conspiracy of several hundred people. Today, currency traders acting alone have twice in one year buried billion dollar trading losses. Hackers have whip-sawed many hundreds of millions of dollars from one bank to another.

Several mainline churches have been the victims of million dollar embezzlements by their leaders. Financial statement frauds abound—Phar-Mor and Leslie Fay immediately come to mind. The fastest growing professional association is the Certified Fraud Examiner's group, which, in five years, swore in 15,000 members. And, forensic accounting is the fastest growing segment of the public accounting profession's new area of practice.

What does all this mean? To us, it means corporate crime is on the rise, but its character is changing. It is moving up the ranks of management and people in positions of trust. A rough guide to the classification of corporate crimes appears in Table 12–1.

Table 12–1   Corporate Crime Classification

1. Crimes against the company
   a. Theft, fraud, embezzlement, and breach of loyalty (e.g., corruption, sabotage by employees)
   b. Fraud perpetrated against the corporation by its vendors, suppliers, contractors, customers, and competitors
   c. Robbery, burglary, hijacking, and extortion by criminal elements
   d. Unfair competition
2. Crimes for the company
   a. Smoothing profits (cooking the books)
      (1) Inflating sales
      (2) Understating expenses
   b. Balance-sheet window dressing
      (1) Overstating assets
      (2) Not recording liabilities
   c. Price fixing
   d. Cheating customers
      (1) Short weights, counts, and measures
      (2) Substitution of cheaper materials
      (3) False advertising
   e. Violating governmental regulations (e.g., EEO, OSHA, environmental standards, securities and tax violations, and so on)
   f. Corruption of customer personnel
   g. Political corruption
   h. Padding costs on government contracts

FRAUD AS A CORPORATE CRIME

For ease of discourse, let us again focus on what is perhaps the most common corporate crime; that is, the crime of fraud (i.e., intentional deception—lying and cheating). Most corporate frauds are not usually discovered in the course of routine financial audits.

Knowledge of the existence of fraud comes to light based on (1) an allegation, complaint, or a rumor of fraud by a third party; (2) an investigator's intuition or general suspicions that something is awry; (3) an auditor's discovery of an accounting discrepancy; (4) an exception from expectation made by a person senior to the suspect—an unacceptable condition (e.g., profits, sales, costs, assets, or liabilities are too low or too high); or (5) the sudden discovery that something—cash, property, reports, files, documents, data, and so on—is missing. Rarely do you know for certain at the outset that a fraud or any crime was in fact committed. In instances of fraud, unless the culprit turns himself or herself in, you do not have a *corpus delicti* before you. At best, you have some rather sketchy information. The first thing to determine is whether a fraud has in fact been committed by making a preliminary investigation.

The objective of any preliminary investigation is to establish what crime has been committed. A crime exists when there is a proven loss of something of value to a victim; a perpetrator who caused that loss; and a law that makes that loss a crime. The immediate facts to determine are whether the following exist:

- A criminal law
- A breach of that law
- A likely perpetrator
- A victim

Evidence to support a conviction under the particular criminal law is then gathered. Such evidence may consist of the testimony of eyewitnesses, confessions of perpetrators, documents, objects that are means and instruments or fruits of the crime, and, perhaps, the testimony of experts. One of those experts may be an accountant or auditor—someone who can explain what the legal significance is of modified or destroyed records, data, documents, and files.

Accounting-type frauds usually are accompanied by the modification, alteration, destruction, or counterfeiting of accounting information. But accounting information can be either intentionally modified, altered, and destroyed, or accidentally modified, altered, or destroyed, such as by human error or omission. The objective for the investigator is to determine whether a discrepancy in accounting records can be attributed to human error. If so, there may be no criminal fraud. If the discrepancy (missing records, destroyed records, modified records, counterfeit records, errors, omissions) cannot be attributed to accident or human error, a full-scale investigation should follow.

Frauds committed within accounting systems (e.g., those frauds where records, reports, and data are destroyed, modified, or counterfeited) can be grouped into the following major categories: (1) Frauds committed for the company, and (2) frauds committed against the company.

Frauds for the company are committed mainly by senior managers who wish to enhance the financial position or condition of the company by ploys such as overstating income, sales, or assets or by understating expenses and liabilities. In essence, an intentional misstatement of a financial fact is committed and that can constitute a civil or criminal fraud. But income, for example, may also be intentionally understated to evade taxes, and expenses can be overstated for a similar reason. Frauds for the company usually are intended by top managers to deceive shareholders, creditors, and regulatory authorities. Similar frauds by lower-level profit-center managers may be intended to deceive their superiors in the organization, to make them (superiors) believe that the unit is more profitable or productive than it is, and thereby, perhaps, to earn a higher bonus award or a promotion for the subordinate manager.

In frauds for the organization, we often find top management involved in a conspiracy to deceive. In frauds against the organization, there may be only one person involved in the fraud (e.g., an accounts payable person who fabricates invoices from a nonexistent vendor, has checks issued to that vendor, which the clerk then converts into cash for his or her own use).

Frauds against the company may also include the bribery of employees by vendors, suppliers, contractors, and competitors. Cases of employee bribery are difficult to discern or discover by audit because a corporation's accounting records generally are not manipulated, altered, or destroyed. Bribe payments are made "under the table," or as lawyers say, *sub rosa*. The first hint of bribery may come from an irate vendor whose product is consistently rejected despite its quality, price, and performance. Bribery also may become apparent if the employee begins to live beyond his or her means—far in excess of salary and family resources. (Beware of the janitor who drives a Rolls Royce, the accounts payable clerk who visits the casinos too frequently, and a purchasing agent who never buys his own lunch.)

If corporate fraud is suspected or if some proof exists, management has several options:

- Cause a deeper audit to be made if the amount of loss appears to be substantial
- Censure or terminate the employee or employees responsible for the loss if the loss is minimal

- File a claim to recover on the loss from the company's fidelity insurance provider
- Request a law enforcement agency to probe into the matter
- Engage a private investigator to probe into the loss and document the case either for bonding claim purposes or for prosecution
- Disregard the loss, if minimal, and then tighten internal controls
- Alert the directors and audit committee of the board

INVESTIGATING CORPORATE CRIME

While a scientist can rely on some permanence in the laws of physics, a detective has no such advantage. Heuristic approaches (trial and error) are the forte of the detective. There is no algorithm for the solution of a crime. The only things immutable in crime discernment are its elements, and these are as follows:

1. There must be a validly enacted law that provides for criminal sanctions if it is breached. That law must be promulgated—made generally known.
2. There must be a perpetrator—someone who has breached the law.
3. The perpetrator must have sufficient legal and mental capacity to understand the nature of his or her act.
4. The breach must be made known to the detective by his or her own faculties and resources or by some third party (i.e., a victim of the breach, a witness to the breach, or someone otherwise knowledgeable about the breach—a confederate of the violator, a paid informer).

Then, the work of the detective is to document the violation of the law with proofs and to gather those proofs in such a manner that the suspect's legal rights are not transgressed. Proofs may consist of confessions given freely by violators, statements from witnesses who observed the criminal act or were its victim, and physical things that relate to the crime (i.e., means, instruments, and fruits of the crime—weapons, tools, writings, clothing, money, books, records, and so on).

The step-by-step process of criminal investigation can be set forth in terms of systems logic, as shown in Table 12–2.

Table 12–2   Criminal Investigation Process

1. A putative criminal act is reported, discovered, or discerned.
   a. Is the act in fact a violation of a criminal law?
   b. If so, what specific law or laws?
   c. When was the act committed (statute of limitations)?
   d. Where was the act committed (jurisdiction, venue)?
   e. How was the act committed (*modus operandi*)?
   f. Who committed the act (legal capacity)?
   g. How can the actor be identified and located (arrest, search and seizure)?
   h. Why was the act committed (motive, intent)?
2. What evidence links the criminal act to the suspect?
   a. Are witnesses to the criminal act available?
      (1) Are these witnesses legally competent, credible, and willing to testify?
      (2) Can they positively identify the suspect?
   b. Are documents to prove the charge available?
      (1) Who has legal custody of these documents?
      (2) Will these documents be surrendered voluntarily or will judicial processes be required (subpoena)?
      (3) Do the documents speak for themselves or will they require a foundation for their introduction (public vs. private records)?
      (4) Are the documents kept in the regular course of trade or business?
   c. Are tools, means, instruments, and fruits of the crime available?
      (1) How were these acquired? (Incident to arrest? Execution of search warrant? Voluntarily submitted? Found at the crime scene? Discovered by accident?)
      (2) Have these items been marked, identified, and kept in a secured place? Has their transfer been recorded as to date, person, and purpose (chain of custody)?
3. Has the suspect been arrested?
   a. With or without a warrant?
4. Was the suspect advised of his or her rights?
5. Was the suspect searched?
   a. Incident to arrest?
6. Was any incriminating evidence found on his or her person or in the immediate area of arrest?
7. Was the suspect interrogated?
   a. Before or after having been advised of his or her rights?
8. Did the suspect make any admissions of guilt?
   a. *Res gestae* statements?
9. Did the suspect make a confession?
   a. Voluntarily?
   b. Were any oral promises of leniency made?
   c. Of intercessions with prosecutorial or judicial authorities?
   d. Any other assurances?

Laws Affecting Evidence Gathering in Internal Investigations

Investigators should be aware of laws restricting certain aspects of investigations and risks of liability arising from the treatment of suspects. Brief descriptions of key legal areas follow. Investigators should always consult with legal counsel regarding specific investigative actions.

> *Malicious Prosecution*—Criminal prosecution instituted maliciously and without probable cause.
>
> *Invasion of Privacy Tort*—Employees and other persons have an expectation of privacy that is recognized by many states. During the course of an investigation, evidence may be sought through searches or examinations of offices, desks, papers, mail, telephone, e-mail, lockers, and so on. Any one of these areas, under certain conditions and if not handled properly, could lead to an invasion of privacy charge.

An organization must deal with the presence of a discrete expectation of privacy with respect to all searches, including electronic files such as e-mail. The organization should promulgate a clear statement on searches and privacy designed to eliminate an employee expectation of privacy and assert employer ownership, authority, and oversight of equipment and materials such as the e-mail system. (See two California cases covering these issues: *Thomasson v. Bank of America* and *Flannigan v. Epson America.*)

Eliminating an expectation of privacy is similar to that of posting search warning signs at building entrances. Persons reading a sign that clearly warns them they can be searched if they enter and exit the building should not expect to invoke a privacy privilege. They have been warned and by entering the building have "consented" to have articles and perhaps their person searched. Of course, they did not give a blanket consent and there are still limits to searches. And, the right to conduct a search, even in a posted area, may be lost if search procedures are lax or nonexistent. Just having a sign or a written policy may not be enough—there must be some implementation of the policy.

Taking e-mail as an example, policies, rules, and actions should clarify that (1) individual access to the e-mail system is via key or password controlled and administered by security or network administrators; (2) the network may be monitored; and (3) e-mail files may be searched and seized at any time and for any reason. Generally speaking, an employer (government or private) may search an employee's computer and peripherals if the employer has common authority over them. The employer must consider whether, under the facts, the employee would expect privacy in those items and whether that expectation would be objectively reasonable. Relevant factors include whether:

1. The area/item to be searched has been set aside for the employee's exclusive or personal use (i.e., does the employee have the only key to the computer or do others have access to the data);
2. The employee has been given permission to store personal information on the system or in the area to be searched;
3. The employee has been advised that the system may be accessed or looked at by others;
4. There have been past inspections of the area/item and this fact is known to the employee;
5. There is an employment policy that states that searches of the work area may be conducted at any time, for any reason;
6. The purpose of the search, if the employer is the federal government, was work-related rather than primarily for law enforcement objectives.

Search and Seizure—A person may waive his or her constitutional right to be secure against unreasonable search by giving consent to search of his or her person, possessions, or premises. For a consent search to be valid: (1) there must be a voluntary consent to search, given without any degree of coercion or made under duress; (2) consent should be given by a person who is in fact authorized to give such consent; and (3) the search does not extend beyond the bounds of the consent given.

Defamation—Defamation could arise from a false accusation of criminal conduct. Libel is defamation by writing; slander is defamation by speech. Both are communication of false information to a third party that injures a person's reputation.

False Imprisonment—This usually means unlawful detention, an unreasonable holding for a period of time with sufficient restraint. This can arise in an interrogation or questioning of a suspect.

Infliction of Emotional Distress—This too may arise out of the questioning of a suspect. The tort definition, however, requires conduct "so outrageous in character, and so extreme in degree, as to go beyond all possible bounds of decency, and to be regarded as atrocious, and utterly intolerable in a civilized community" (Restatement [Second] of Torts, Section 46, Comment d [1965].)

When interviewing personnel who may be questioned later by law enforcement or government investigators, be aware of the potential legal traps in obstruction of justice and witness tampering laws. The key statute is the Victim and Witness Protection Act of the U.S. Code (18 U.S.C., Section 1512). The witness tampering provision, which prohibits the knowing use of physical force, threats, corrupt persuasion, or any misleading conduct* that would "influence, delay, or prevent the testimony of any person in an official proceeding" or, cause or induce a person to withhold testimony, records, or documents, or destroy such material, from an official proceeding. The other obstruction of justice statutes deal with influencing or intimidating any juror or court official (18 U.S.C., Section 1503); similar prohibitions are given for impeding legal proceedings before any department or agency of the United States. (18 U.S.C., Section 1505).

Using the Lie Detector in Internal Investigations

Internal investigations are becoming a hazardous undertaking for employers and using a polygraph or lie detector in furtherance of the investigation raises privacy issues and potential liabilities. This is one area where knowledge of the law is mandatory because the burden is on the employer to show justification and proper use of lie detection. There are state and federal laws covering lie detection; we will discuss the federal statute on use of lie detectors here.

The Employee Polygraph Protection Act of 1988 (29 U.S.C., Sections 2001–2008) prohibits the use of "lie detectors," which includes a polygraph, deceptograph, voice stress analyzer, psycho-

---

Misleading conduct is defined as making a false statement, intentionally omitting information from a statement, submitting a false or forged writing or recording, or using a trick, scheme, or artifice to mislead.

logical stress evaluator, or "any similar device for the purpose of rendering a diagnostic opinion regarding the honesty or dishonesty of an individual." It is unlawful to (1) make any employee or perspective employee take a lie detector test; (2) use or get the results of any lie detector test of an employee; (3) discharge or take disciplinary action or discriminate against any current or prospective employee who refuses to take a lie detector test, or who fails a lie detector test, or who files a complaint under this law.

The law lays out the rights of the examinee, how the test should be conducted, qualifications and requirements of examiners, and disclosure of test results. Violations of this law carry a civil penalty of not more than $10,000. However, the employer is open to civil actions by the employee and may be liable for back pay and benefits, court costs, and employee's attorney's fees. The statute of limitations is three years after the date of the alleged violation. There are a number of exemptions under the law, including the following:

- Government employees
- Defense Department contractors and consultants
- Intelligence or counterintelligence personnel, consultants, or contractors
- Firms and agencies involved in ongoing investigations, providing the employee is thought to be involved in an economic crime, and the employer details in a statement to the examinee the reasons for the test.

There are limited exemptions to: private security companies engaged in armored car services, alarm security systems installers, utilities security, public transportation security, currency and precious commodities personnel, and controlled substance manufacturers or distributors.

To be regarded as an "ongoing investigation," the investigation must deal with a specific incident and an "economic loss or injury" must have occurred. An investigation, therefore, cannot be part of a sustained surveillance program, and the loss must have happened and be documented via report, audit, or initial incident investigation. The economic loss could result from theft, embezzlement, fraud, or industrial espionage or sabotage.

Employees who had access to the property under investigation and of whom the employer has a "reasonable suspicion" may be subject to lie detector/polygraph testing. The individual conducting the polygraph testing must have a valid and current state license and be bonded.

Note again, through all of this, that the burden is on the employer to show that all the various elements exist to conduct polygraph tests. Thus, employers are urged to consult with legal counsel prior to using lie detection testing.

Rules of Evidence

A court trial is intended to deduce the truth of a given proposition. In a criminal case, the proposition is the guilt or innocence of an accused. The evidence introduced and received by the court to prove the charge must be beyond a reasonable doubt, not necessarily to a moral certainty, but that quantity and quality of evidence which would convince an honest and reasonable layman that the defendant is guilty after all the evidence is considered and weighed impartially. The level of proof in a civil case, by contrast, requires only a "preponderance of the evidence."

But what is evidence and how can it be weighed and introduced? In a broad sense, *evidence* is anything perceptible by the five senses and any form of species of proof, such as testimony of witnesses, records, documents, facts, data, or concrete objects, legally presented at a trial to prove a contention and induce a belief in the minds of the court or jury. In weighing evidence, the court or jury may consider such things as the demeanor of a witness, any bias for or against an accused, and any relationship to the accused. So, evidence can be testimonial, circumstantial, demonstrative, inferential, and even theoretical when given by a qualified expert. Evidence is simply anything that proves or disproves any matter in question.

To be legally acceptable as evidence, however, testimony, documents, objects, or facts must be competent, relevant, and material to the issues being litigated and be gathered in a lawful manner. Otherwise, on the motion by the opposite side, the evidence may be excluded. Now, perhaps, we should elaborate on relevancy, materiality, and competency: "Relevancy of evidence does not depend upon the conclusiveness of the testimony offered, but upon its legitimate tendency to establish a controverted fact" (*ICC v. Baird*, 194 U.S. 25, 24 S. Ct. 563, 48 L. Ed. 860).

Some of the evidentiary matters considered relevant and, therefore, admissible are:

1. The motive for the crime
2. The ability of the defendant to commit the crime
3. The opportunity to commit the crime
4. Threats or expressions of ill will by the accused
5. The means of committing the offense (possession of a weapon, tools, or skills used in committing the crime)
6. Physical evidence at the scene linking the accused to the crime
7. The suspect's conduct and comments at the time of arrest
8. The attempt to conceal identity
9. The attempt to destroy evidence
10. Valid confessions

Although the motive for a crime is not an element of necessary proof to sustain a conviction (but criminal intent usually is), motive is important to the investigator because it tends to identify the more likely suspects when the actual culprit is unknown. The motive also helps to construct a "theory of the case"; that is, the who, what, when, where, how, and why of the crime. So, motive should not be discounted just because it is not an element of proof of a crime. Motive and motivation can narrow the search for the culprit and can be a substantial aid in reconstructing the crime (building a theory of the case).

As a general rule, crime motivations can be separated into four major categories: (1) economic, (2) egocentric, (3) ideological, and (4) psychotic. A psychotic motivation can be an impairment to successful criminal prosecution (e.g., an insanity plea). Of the other three motivations, the economic motivation is the most common. The criminal wants or needs more money or more wealth. Egocentric motivation means the criminal wants more prestige, more recognition, higher social or political status, or even a job promotion. Ideological motivation means the criminal feels his or her cause or life is morally superior to that of the victim, or feels exploited, abused, or discriminated against by the victim.

The materiality rule requires that evidence must have an important value to a case or prove a point in issue. Unimportant details only extend the period of time for trial. Accordingly, a trial court judge may rule against the introduction of evidence that is repetitive or additive (merely proves the same point in another way), or evidence that tends to be remote, even though relevant. Materiality then is the degree of relevancy. The court cannot become preoccupied with trifles or unnecessary details. For example, the physical presence of a suspect in the computer room or tape library or near a terminal on the day when a spurious transaction was generated may be relevant and material. His or her physical presence in a non-computer-related area of the building may be relevant, but immaterial.

Competency of evidence means that which is adequately sufficient, reliable, and relevant to the case and presented by a qualified and capable (and sane) witness (i.e., the presence of those characteristics, or the absence of those disabilities, that render a witness legally fit and qualified to give testimony in a court, applied in the same sense to documents or other forms of written evidence). But competency differs from credibility. Competency is a question that arises before considering the evidence given by a witness; credibility refers to the degree of credit to be given to testimony. The former denotes the personal qualifications of a witness; the latter, the witness's veracity. Competency is for the judge to determine; credibility is for the jury to decide.

The competency rule also dictates that conclusions or opinions of a nonexpert witness on matters that require technical expertise be excluded. For example, testimony on the cause of death by an investigating officer may not be appropriate or "competent" in a trial for murder or wrongful death, because he or she is not qualified by education, study, and experience to make such an assessment. Testifying that there were "no visible signs of life" when the body was found may be acceptable, however.

When an expert witness is called on to testify, a foundation must be laid before testimony can be accepted or allowed. Laying a foundation means that the witness's expertise needs to be established before any professional opinion is rendered. Qualifying a witness as an expert means demonstrating to the judge's satisfaction that by formal education, advanced study, and experience, the witness is knowledgeable about the topic on which his or her testimony will bear. The testimony of experts is an exception to the so-called hearsay rule.

The *hearsay* rule is based on the theory that testimony that is a repetition of what some other person said should not be admitted because of the possibility of distortion or misunderstanding. Furthermore, an exception implies that the actual witness who made the statement is unavailable for cross-examination and has not been sworn in as a witness. Generally speaking, witnesses can testify only to those things they have personal and direct knowledge of, not conclusions or opinions. But there are occasions—exceptions—when hearsay evidence is admissible, including the following:

1. Dying declarations, either verbal or written
2. Valid confessions
3. Tacit admissions
4. Public records that do not require an opinion—they speak for themselves
5. *Res gestae* statements—spontaneous explanations, if spoken as part of the criminal act or immediately following the commission of such criminal act
6. Former testimony given under oath
7. Business entries—made in the regular course of doing business

Photocopies of original business documents and other writings and printed matter are often made to preserve evidence. These are used by the investigator so that original records needed to run a business are not removed and to ensure that in the event of an inadvertent destruction of such originals, a certified, true copy of the document is still available as proof. The certified copy also may be used by the investigator to document his or her case report. At the trial, however, the original document—if still available—is the "best evidence" and must be presented. *Best evidence* in this context means primary evidence, not secondary; original as distinguished from substitutionary; the highest evidence for the nature of the case that is acceptable (i.e., a written instrument is itself always regarded as the primary or best possible evidence of its existence and contents); a copy, or the recollection of a witness, would be secondary evidence (*Manhattan Malting Company v. Swetland*, 14 Mont. 269, 36 P. 84). Contents of a document must be proved by producing the document itself (*Nunan v. Timberlake*, 85 F.2d 407, 66 App. D.C. 150).

Elaboration on Heresay Exceptions

In an idealistic sense, a court trial is a quest to determine the truth; however, the means of acquiring evidence are clearly variable. Some means are legal, others are illegal (e.g., violate constitutional guarantees against unreasonable search and seizure, forced confessions, failure to be represented by counsel, and so on). Realistically therefore, a court trial can result only in a degree of probability of the truth and not in absolute truth in the philosophic sense.

In the Anglo-American tradition, witnesses, other than experts, cannot generally testify as to probabilities, opinions, assumptions, impressions, generalizations, or conclusions, but can testify only as to things, people, and events they have seen, felt, tasted, smelled, or heard first-hand. And, even those things must be legally and logically relevant. Logical relevancy means the evidence being offered must tend to prove or disprove a fact of consequence. But even if logically relevant, a court may exclude evidence if it is likely to inflame or confuse a jury, or consume too much time. In addition, testimony as to the statistical probability of guilt is considered too prejudicial and unreliable to be accepted.

Testimony as to the character and reputation of an accused may be admissible under certain conditions, even though it would seem to violate the hearsay rule. Such testimony may be admitted where character (i.e., the mental condition or legal competency of the accused) is an element of the action. Evidence of other crimes committed by an accused generally is not admissible to prove character. It may, however, be admitted for other purposes (e.g., as proof of motive, opportunity, intent, preparation, scheme, or plan to commit an act).

The credibility of a witness may be attacked or supported by evidence of reputation, but subject to several limitations (i.e., the evidence may refer only to character for truthfulness or untruthfulness, and only if the witness's character for truthfulness was previously challenged in the trial). A witness's credibility may also be attacked by a showing that he or she was convicted of a serious crime (punishable by death or imprisonment for more than a year) or for other crimes such as theft, dishonesty, or false statement. Such conviction should have occurred in the recent past—usually within the last ten years.

Evidence can be direct or circumstantial. *Direct evidence* proves a fact directly; that is, if the evidence is believed, the fact is established. *Circumstantial evidence* proves the desired fact indirectly and depends on the strength of the inferences raised by the evidence.

For example, a letter properly addressed, stamped, and mailed is assumed (inferred) to have been received by its addressee. Testimony that a letter was so addressed, stamped, and mailed raises an inference that it was received. The inference may, however, be rebutted by testimony that it, in fact, was not received.

The *best evidence rule* deals with written documents proffered as evidence. The rule requires that the original, not a copy thereof, be presented at the trial, if available. If the original has been destroyed or is in the hands of an opposite party and not subject to legal process by search warrant or subpoena, then an authenticated copy can be substituted. Business records and documents kept in the ordinary course of business can be presented as evidence too, even though the person who made entries or prepared the documents is unavailable.

Chain of Custody

When evidence in the form of a document or object (means or instrument) is seized at a crime scene, as a result of *subpoena duces tecum*, or discovered in the course of audit and investigation, it should be marked, identified, inventoried, and preserved to maintain it in its original condition and to establish a clear chain of custody until it is introduced at the trial. If gaps in possession or custody occur, the evidence may be challenged at the trial on the theory that the writing or object introduced may not be original or is not in its original condition and, therefore, of doubtful authenticity.

For a seized document to be admissible as evidence, it is necessary to prove that it is the same document that was seized and that it is in the same condition as it was when seized. Because several persons may handle it in the interval between seizure and the trial of the case, evidence should be adequately marked at the time of seizure for later identification, and its custody must be shown from that time until it is introduced in court.

An investigator or auditor who seizes or secures documents should at once identify them by some marking so that he or she can later testify that they are the documents seized, and that they are in the same condition as when they were seized. The investigator may, for instance, put his or her initials and the date of seizure in the margin, in a corner, or at some other inconspicuous place on the front or back of each document. If circumstances indicate that such marking may render the document subject to attack on the grounds that it has been defaced or is not in the same condition as when seized, the investigator or auditor may, after making a copy for comparison or for use as an exhibit to his or her report, put the document into an envelope, write a description and any other identifying information on the front of the envelope, and then seal the envelope.

These techniques should be used any time an investigator or auditor comes into possession of an original document which may be needed as evidence in a trial. If you make copy of documentary evidence, steps should be taken to preserve the copy's authenticity in case it is needed as secondary evidence in case the original document is not available for the trial.

Secondary Evidence

To be able to introduce secondary evidence, absence of the original document must be explained satisfactorily to the court. Secondary evidence is not restricted to photocopies of the document. It may consist of testimony of witnesses or transcripts of the document's contents. Although the federal courts give no preference to the type of secondary evidence, the majority of other jurisdictions do.

Under the majority rule, testimony (parol) evidence will not be allowed to prove the contents of a document if secondary documentary evidence is available to prove its contents. However, before secondary evidence of the original document can be introduced, the party offering the contents of the substitute must have used all reasonable and diligent means to obtain the original. Again, this is a matter to be determined by the court. When the original document has been destroyed by the party attempting to prove its contents, secondary evidence still will be admitted if the destruction was in the ordinary course of business, or by mistake, or even intentionally—provided it was not done for any fraudulent purpose.

Privileged Communications

The rule supporting privileged communications is based on the belief that it is necessary to maintain the confidentiality of certain communications. It only covers those communications that are a unique product of the protected relationship. The basic reason behind these protected communications is the belief that the protection of certain relationships is more important to society than the possible harm resulting from the loss of such evidence. Legal jurisdictions vary as to what communications are protected. Here is a list of some of the more prevalent privileged relationships:

1. Attorney-client
2. Husband-wife
3. Physician-patient
4. Accountant-client (but not in all jurisdictions and not in federal tax matters)
5. Priest-penitent
6. Law enforcement–informant
7. News reporters and their sources may have a limited privilege under shield laws enacted in most states.

When dealing with privileged communications, the following basic principles should be considered:

1. Only the holder of a privilege, or someone authorized by the holder, can assert the privilege.
2. If the holder fails to assert it after having notice and an opportunity to assert it, the privilege is waived.
3. The privilege also may be waived if the holder discloses a significant part of the communication to a party not within the protected relationship.
4. The communication, to be within the privilege, must be sufficiently related to the relationship protected (e.g., communications between an attorney and client must be related to legal consultations).

It should be noted that under common law, one spouse cannot testify against the other spouse in a criminal trial; while married, neither may waive this testimonial incompetency. This witness incompetency must be distinguished from the confidential communications between spouses made and completed during the marriage that retain the privileged status after the marriage has ceased. Like other such privileges, conversations in the known presence of third parties do not fall within the protected communications rule. Protected communications are those that are, in fact, confidential or induced by the marriage relation. Ordinary conversations relating to matters of business of such a nature as to be deemed not confidential are not within the purview of the privilege.

The laws of different states vary widely in the application of the principles of privileged communications. Depending on what protected relationship is involved, different rules may apply regarding what communications are protected, the methods of waiver, and the duration of the privilege. Whenever you are confronted with the need to use evidence in the nature of communications between parties in one of the relationships listed before, consultation with an attorney is advisable, especially if the evidence is crucial to the case.

ACCOUNTANTS AND AUDITORS AS EXPERT WITNESSES

Accountants and auditors are often called on to provide testimony in criminal prosecutions where their services were utilized to support investigations of such crimes as financial frauds, embezzlement, misapplication of funds, arson for profit, bankruptcy fraud, improper accounting practices, tax evasion, and so on. Accountants and auditors also may be used as defense witnesses or as support to the defendant's counsel on matters that involve accounting or auditing issues.

Qualifying accountants and auditors as technical experts is generally not a difficult task. Questions are posed to them concerning their professional credentials (e.g., education, work experience, licensing or certification, technical training courses taken, technical books and journal articles written, offices held in professional associations, awards and commendations received). Usually, smart defense lawyers are not prone to challenge the expertise of accountants and auditors, assuming they meet at least minimum standards of professional competence. To do so may give these experts an opportunity to fully highlight their professional credentials and perhaps make a greater impression on the jury or judge, thereby adding more weight to their testimony. So, defense attorneys often pass on the opportunity to challenge these expert witnesses.

In general, what accountants and auditors testify to are their audit findings if called by the prosecution; if called by the defense, they testify about the quality of the audit or the opinions expressed by the prosecution's accounting expert in an attempt to create doubt in the jury's mind about the credibility or weight to be given to the prosecution's expert.

To become a "credible" expert accounting witness, one must be generally knowledgeable in his or her own field by education and experience, be a member in good standing of the profession, and, perhaps, be recognized as an authority in that profession or some specialized aspect of practice within that profession that is pertinent to the case at hand. But there are other considerations as well in making an expert a credible witness. Table 12–3 contains some tips in that regard.

Table 12–3   Basics of Being an Expert Accounting Witness

- Speak clearly and audibly
- Refrain from using professional jargon
- Use simple terms to describe findings and opinions rather than overly complex terms
- Speak to the specific questions asked and do not go off on tangents or volunteer more than the question requires
- Do not verbally fence with the defense attorney or prosecutor
- Look directly at the question poser—prosecutor or defense counsel
- Maintain a professional demeanor—do not smile gratuitously at the judge, jury, the lawyer who hired you, or the opponent's counsel
- Be calm and deliberate in responding to questions—speak neither too slowly nor rapid-fire
- Wear conservative clothing—a business suit or dress of neutral tone (gray or dark blue); for men, dark shoes (shined) and socks and a conservative tie properly knotted at the collar (not skewed)
- Be clean and have hair (and beard) neatly combed and perhaps professionally styled
- Use graphs, charts, and other visual aids if they help to clarify a point
- Do not read from notes if you can avoid it. (The opposition lawyer will probably demand to see such notes if you do, and you will then look like you rehearsed your testimony—and did so rather badly.)
- If you have documents to introduce, have them organized so that you can quickly retrieve them when asked to do so by the counsel whose side you are testifying for
- Do not "hem and haw" or stammer; recover your composure when a tough or complex question is posed
- Ask for a repetition or clarification of the question if you do not fully comprehend it
- If you do not know the answer, say so—do not guess
- In cross-examination, do not respond too quickly; counsel for your side may wish to interpose an objection to the question
- If the judge or jury elect to ask a question, respond to it by looking at the questioner
- Do not stare off into space, at the floor, or at the ceiling
- Be friendly to all sides
- Do not raise your voice in anger if the opponent's lawyer tries to bait you
- Be honest. Be honest. Be honest. Don't invent. Don't inflate. Don't be evasive.

A NOTE ON APPENDIX MATERIALS

The schematics, checklists, and forms in this chapter's appendices are tools to help gather information and evidence logically, easier, and more quickly. Some of the forms should help you identify the right persons to be interviewed or who possess or control access to critical items such as documents, schedules, or reports; other forms can help you lay out areas to be investigated. The following are more detailed descriptions of and suggestions for using some of the materials presented here:

> *Internal Corporate Investigation Flowchart*—Where to start an internal investigation is the first thing an investigator needs to know; how it will play out can only be conjectured at the outset. Because there is never a completed roadmap at the start of an investigation, we offer the accompanying flowchart as an aid to help determine where to begin an investigation, as well as to provide a visual guide to the various possible paths an internal inquiry can take. The flowchart can be viewed as a conceptual map for analyzing findings and for possible actions associated with the internal investigation.
>
> *Organizational Control Chart*—This chart can be used to identify employees and their duties, which may be part of a relevant function under investigation; linking duties with names can help locate documents and select those to be interviewed.
>
> *Scattergraph*—A scattergraph is a visual tool that can be used to quickly identify weaknesses in a manual/computerized system. The graph is used to summarize functions performed by employees within an organization. Job functions should be listed along the right side; employee names would be listed at the top of the form. An "X" would then be marked in the box that matches the employee or employees (or suspects) with the function performed. On completion of the scattergraph, each employee column should be evaluated to determine any potential weaknesses or to flag possible primary suspects.

APPENDIX 12-1

Investigation Flowchart

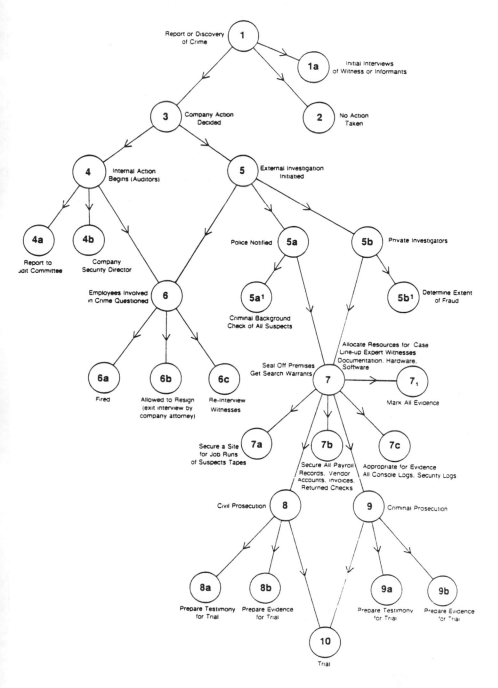

APPENDIX 12-2 Organizational Control Chart

Instructions for Completion

List under the heading "Duties" each of the key tasks or duties
necessary to carry out the function. Under the heading "Employee
Name or position Title," identify each person that has a part in
the performance of this function. Then, by placing a check mark
in the appropriate column, indicate which employee(s) performs
each of the duties listed.

Duties	Employee Name or Position Title													

APPENDIX 12–3

Engaging Technical Assistance at the Investigative Planning Stage

Selection of technical consultant or expert witness—critical preliminary information:

- Resume or curriculum vitae
- Scope of retention
- Estimate of number of hours to complete the job
- Hourly compensation rate
- Whether a consultant or a trial witness

Preliminary analysis of books and records to determine:

- Possible needs for proof
- Relevancy and validity of documents
- Extent of evidence gathering necessary
- Review of the case's merit and legal theories

The Forensic Accountant can assist legal counsel in:

- Detecting the nature and extent of the crime
- Refining and improving case theory
- Developing an overall theory of the case
- Developing a working case strategy
- Conducting feasibility study in advance of preliminary investigation
- Conducting cost-benefit analysis in advance of embarking on major case investigation
- Identifying case's strengths and weaknesses
- Identifying and describing the organization's financial information system
- Specifying facts to be obtained during discovery
- Drafting interrogatories, document production requests, questionnaires
- Preparing technical questions for preliminary interviews of witnesses and taking depositions
- Identifying documents to be searched for

continued

APPENDIX 12-3   *cont.*

- Preparing search warrants and subpoenas
- Advising on methods of obtaining complex evidence intact
- Interpreting complex data and accounting evidence
- Indexing case intelligence and subpoenaed evidence
- Explaining intricacies of victim's operations
- Explaining applications/vulnerabilities of victim's financial system and security measures
- Constructing probable *modus operandi*
- Focusing on the suspect(s) and advising on probable means, motives, and opportunity
- Advising on patterns of known computer abuse in a given industry
- Conducting investigator orientation sessions on basics of computer processing and its applications in victim's industry or field
- Preparing intelligence bulletins for staff on new developments in the case
- Preparing assessments for costs, damages, and recovery

APPENDIX 12-4 Information Gathering Form

CHIEF INVESTIGATOR	PAGE	OF	DATE	CASE NAME				CASE NUMBER

REF. NO.	QUESTION TO BE ANSWERED	INFORMATION REQUIRED TO ANSWER QUESTION	LIKELY SOURCE OF INFORMATION	INFORMATION GATHERING TECHNIQUE	INFORMATION MEDIA	ASSIGNED TO AND DATE	EVIDENCE I.D. TAG NUMBER	COMMENTS

INFORMATION GATHERING GUIDE

APPENDIX 12-5 Investigation Planning Form

CHIEF INVESTIGATOR	PAGE	OF	DATE	CASE NAME				CASE NUMBER

INVESTIGATION ACTIVITY TASK						
REF #	DESCRIPTION	RESPONSIBILITY	START DATE	PLAN END DATE	COMMENTS	

ADDITIONAL COMMENTS

PREPARED BY	WITNESSED BY

APPENDIX 12–6

Worksheet for Information Gathering

CHIEF INVESTIGATOR	PAGE OF DATE	CASE NAME	CASE NUMBER

Dept. ————

Account. ————

Section. ————

NAME AND FUNCTION OR TITLE

DUTY / OR ACTIVITY							COMMENTS

APPENDIX 12–7
Scattergraph

CHIEF INVESTIGATOR	PAGE OF	CASE NAME		CASE NUMBER
	DATE			

Internal and External
Sources of Information
- Person's name
- Department name
- Organization's name

INFORMATION SOURCES

Types of Information
- Forms   ● Records
- Flowcharts
- Cancelled checks
- Coding sheets
- Source listings, etc.

- Documentation
- Magnetic files
- Internal Records
- External Records

CATEGORY OF INFORMATION	INFORMATION							COMMENTS

PLANNING WORKSHEET FOR INFORMATION GATHERING

APPENDIX 12-8
Sample Search Consent Form

You are hereby advised that it is our desire to search the [premises, object, etc.] _____

located at _____
for the purpose of investigating the [insert specific incident or reason] _____

that occurred on said [premises] on _____.
Before we search your [premises], we wish to advise you that you have the following rights:

1. You have the absolute right to refuse to voluntarily permit us to enter and search the [premises].
2. You have the right to require us to secure a search warrant prior to our conducting any search.
3. You also may voluntarily permit us to enter and search your [premises] and, in such event, any incriminating evidence that we find may be used against you in any proceeding.
4. If you agree to voluntarily consent to an entry and search of the [premises], you may revoke such consent at any time.

I have read the above and been advised of my rights

regarding a search of _____.
I hereby state that I fully understand my stated rights. I do hereby waive any search warrant requirement and

consent to allow _____ and _____,

who have identified themselves to me as _____
to enter and search my [premises] as often as may be necessary and to inspect, photograph, and/or seize any items which they may deem relevant. This waiver and consent is being given by me voluntarily and without threats or promises of any kind.

Name _____

Address _____

Date _____ Time _____

Officer/Name _____

APPENDIX 12–9
Sample Format for a Confession

STATE OF _____
COUNTY OF _____, SS.

BEFORE ME, the undersigned, a notary public, in and for the state and county aforesaid, person-

ally appeared _____, who being duly sworn according to law, did depose and say as follows:

1. My name is _____ , and I reside

   at _____.

2. I have been employed by the _____

   [Company] since ____, most recently as _____

   _____ at _____.

3. Before making any statement, I was advised by

   _____, a representative of the

   _____ [Company] that:

   a. I am not obligated to make any statement whatsoever with respect to matters here-inafter set forth.
   b. I am entitled to consult with and be repre-sented by an attorney before and during the making of any statement by me.
   c. Any statement I make may be used in evidence in any civil or criminal proceeding which may be commenced against me.

4. I am making this statement of my own free will without threat or coercion made or offered directly or indirectly and with a full under-standing of my rights as aforesaid, and I hereby expressly waive my right to remain

APPENDIX 12–9 *cont.*

silent and to consult with or be represented
by counsel in connection herewith. I have not
been offered or promised, directly or indirectly, anything of value in limiting the gen-
erality of the foregoing, any promise on the

part of the _____
[Company] from instituting any criminal information or proceeding under applicable state or
federal law.

5. The facts relating to this matter are as follows:

   _____

   _____

   _____

6. This statement was given by me orally in the

   presence of _____, a representative

   of the _____ [Company] and was reduced to

   writing by _____.

7. I have read the foregoing, and the same is
   true, correct, and complete and is adopted and
   affirmed by me. I have further initialed each
   page for identification.

SWORN TO and subscribed before me this _____

day of _____ 19__.

_____
Notary Public

My Commission Expires: _____

13

Reporting Fraud

The Fraud Reporting Form in Figure 13–1 presents a suggested format to use for a final report to document actions surrounding a fraud incident. As with any investigative reporting form, you should consult with legal counsel before using it within your organization. The report form has been designed to fulfill three purposes:

1. To provide a format for recording the essential details of a fraud.
2. To afford the preparer with a framework for analyzing the fraud case.
3. To develop improved management and security policies to detect and prevent fraud.

The form covers various elements of a fraud, including computer-related fraud. In reporting a fraud incident, it is necessary to be precise. The investigation, as well as the reporting, must proceed as if the outcome will be litigated. Recording exact times, dates, names of persons, and specific descriptions of evidence are critical in a civil or criminal investigation or litigation. In short, stick to facts; discount hearsay, rumor, or opinion; and record only what is relevant

Model Fraud Reporting Form

Title_____Report Number_____
Company_____Division_____
Prepared by_____Date_____

Personal Information
Name_____Title_____
Department_____Salary_____Age____Sex_____
Years/months with Company_____Marital Status_____
Home address_____
City_____State____Zip_____Phone_____
Background/position:_____

Description of suspect(s)/accomplice(s), if any:_____

Relationship to perpetrator and Company:_____

Specifics of Incident
Date and duration of incident: Start date:_____
End date:_____
Nature of incident:_____

Incident location (give department and operation involved):_____

If data processing system involved, what specific equipment, application programs, or operating systems were manipulated or abused:_____

How was the fraud perpetrated?_____

Loss Information
Direct loss (estimation or precise dollar value):_____

Organization time loss:_____

Describe equipment or other items lost and give total and individual dollar values:_____

Figure 13–1   Model Fraud Reporting Form

Description of Investigation

How was the incident discovered (audit. informer. accidental discovery)?_____
_____
_____

How was the incident investigated?_____
_____
_____
_____
_____

Describe the evidence gathered:_____
_____
_____

Describe the perpetrator and/or suspect(s) interview:_____
_____
_____

Is a copy of employee/perpetrator statement attached? ☐ Yes ☐ No

Disposition of the Case

If legal action was taken. supply the following information:

   a. Case citation:_____
   b. Location (court. city. county. state):_____
   c. Documents prepared in case:

      ☐ Complaint   ☐ Trial Transcript
      ☐ Search Warrant   ☐ Sentencing Report
      ☐ Preliminary Hearing   ☐ Probation Report
      ☐ Crime Report   ☐ Other Documents (including comments on
      ☐ Points and Authorities   any of the above from drafters. opposition.
      ☐ Laboratory Report   and attorneys)

Comments on the above:_____
_____
_____

Disposition of the incident (other than legal: i.e.. no charge filed. restitution. employee(s) dismissed:
_____
_____

Identify and give dollar values for items recovered:_____
_____
_____

Comments on security. control. audit or management weakness relevant to this case:_____
_____
_____
_____

Recommended corrective actions to prevent further incidents:_____
_____
_____

Case history reviewed by:_____Date_____
Signature_____

to the cause of the incident and its effect. Always keep in mind: Your every word may be repeated or read at an eventual trial.

DISCOVERING FRAUD

Most frauds are uncovered by accident or luck, through an informant, or during the course of an audit. Once discovered, however, many organizations simply do not know what to do. The following suggestions offer guidance for developing a plan of action to handle a fraud incident.

Fraud Reporting Policy

A policy directive from corporate management should first clarify when to report a fraud, under what circumstances, and to whom. As discussed in the previous chapters, corporate management must take the lead for several reasons. First, in any company with multiple divisions or offices scattered around the country, local management will have neither the experience nor the training to deal with a fraud incident. And, they may not be impartial toward the suspects or may have reasons for not wanting any incident to be reported to corporate headquarters.

A reporting policy sets up a formal system for handling fraud incidents as well as giving management another form of control over corporatewide activities. When to report—immediately on confirmation of suspicions or when at least there is reasonable certainty that a possible criminal or damaging act has occurred? If local managers wait too long to report an incident, evidence may be lost or suspects may leave. The report should be directed to corporate headquarters and either the director of internal audit or legal counsel.

Initial Actions

On notification, audit or security personnel should meet with local managers to determine whether the case is open-and-shut or unsupported and if the evidence is sufficient or further investigation is necessary. At this stage, a potential fraud should be handled primarily as a business problem rather than a legal problem, which may come later.

Interim Reports

The first interim report should describe the case review and determine whether the incident deserves further investigation. Subsequent reports should give the status of the investigation—the suspects, authorities contacted, evidence gathered, and possible outcome (i.e., legal, civil, restitution, and so on).

The Final Report

The report form in Figure 13–1 has more than thirty questions for documenting a fraud incident. All the information to fill out may not be essential in every case. The following paragraphs provide more detail on the questions in the form.

Personal Information   Give a precise and appropriate description of the perpetrator, especially job function and, if it is a computer-related fraud, EDP duties and experience. The same applies to suspects or accomplices, if any, and their relationship to the perpetrator and the company.

Dates and Time   Because an incident may take place over several months, the time or duration of the incident is very important. Again, be precise; however, if exact dates are not known, give approximate time frame.

Description of the Incident   Be specific about the incident (i.e., was it a larceny, embezzlement, defalcation, forgery, concealment, misappropriation, malfeasance, or another kind of fraud or theft?). If it is a computer-related incident, give a specific description for the act, such as malicious mischief; theft of data; manipulation of data; unauthorized use of service, software, or hardware; or misuse of copyrighted software programs.

The nature of the incident, which laws were violated, may be difficult to define at first, but by the final report, legal counsel should have it defined. The possibility that several laws may have been broken should always be considered; or, that there may be an applicable law that is not apparent at the outset.

Where the Fraud Occurred   A description of where the incident occurred should give the division, department, and operation plus the specific process or transaction area such as procurement (specifically, purchasing, receiving, or accounts payable), payroll, receivables, and so on.

If the incident involved data processing, be specific in your descriptions of the data processing operation, computer system, the programs, or equipment involved. Remember, in court you may have to show how the system operated normally in order to prove that a manipulation occurred. And, in what computer environment—the user environment, computer room, data preparation area, tape library, input/output desk, or communications room—did the incident happen?

How the Fraud Was Perpetrated   Here you must describe exactly where, within the operation or a particular system, the incident occurred and how the manipulation, collusion, or abuse was accomplished.

Loss Information and Estimates   Estimating, with some precision, the dollar-value loss can be critical in establishing the incident category or for possible future recovery action in a civil suit. If the loss is essentially information, an asset valuation can be prepared by determining (1) the initial purchase cost or internal development costs, (2) enhancements and ongoing costs, or (3) what it would cost to replace the information.

Data processing loss estimates can be based on computer time loss; organization time loss, to include total and estimated dollar value and time/dollar loss of various departments or activities such as program reruns, reviews, corrections, reconstruction, and so on; and individual items or equipment lost.

Incident Discovery   How the incident was discovered can have important consequences for both the investigation and prosecution. If the incident was discovered during an audit, you can use the documentation generated by the audit and have the auditor as a technical advisor or expert witness. If you were tipped by an informer, you have to consider reliability and motives.

Incident Investigation   Give a concise and accurate description of the investigative process, personnel, and authorities contacted (e.g., security, internal auditor, legal counsel, or law enforcement).

Evidence   Describe all evidence that demonstrated the perpetrator's intention to commit a specific criminal act; indicate the collector and custodian of specific evidence and where it is preserved.

Interviews   Include the name of the interviewer, who was interviewed, and the time and date; also summarize key points of the interview and give the names of witnesses present.

Remember, any statement or confession of an employee/perpetrator must be voluntary—no threats or promises; and any confession must be handwritten, dated, and signed. Witnesses should be present during interviews and statement signings.

Case Disposition   The final actions taken by the organization may be legal or civil, or both. Final comments on case disposition should indicate the current employment status of the perpetrator, whether suspended, resigned, terminated, or whereabouts unknown; and if restitution arrangements have been made.

Security and Controls   Describe the security or control systems or procedures that were compromised in carrying out the fraud. If the cause was weak controls or lax management, give an objective appraisal of the problem and personnel involved.

Corrective Actions   Answer these questions: How could this incident have been prevented? What specific security and audit policies, procedures, personnel, or equipment should be improved or added to guard against fraud?

14

Internal Corporate Compliance Investigations

Internal corporate compliance investigations are becoming a necessary, but increasingly hazardous operation. Legal and regulatory mandates are calling for voluntary disclosures, compliance reviews, audits, and investigations to uncover suspected wrongdoing. Coupled with this is a trend to criminalize regulations that were once essentially civil.

Today, organizations are faced with both reporting possible criminal misconduct and lessened standards of criminal liability. Prosecution once hinged on the concept of intent, but this has often been replaced by evidence of "willful blindness," "recklessness," "failure to perceive (a risk)," or "collective knowledge" for corporate liability. Added to this could be the expensive prospect of collateral prosecution and litigation, or being twice charged, tried, and possibly fined or sentenced for a single violation. While legal costs can be exorbitant, litigation can also adversely affect public perception of a company; harm employee, customer, and investor relations; and damage credit lines.

The U.S. Sentencing Commission guidelines have literally changed the conduct of corporate internal investigations, particularly, how and when investigations are initiated, who directs them, when and what results of the investigation are disclosed to the government, and the power of the prosecutor to define the extent of the corporation's cooperation with the government. The guidelines require that once an offense has been discovered, though not fully verified, the organization must start an internal investigation to determine if the incident should be reported to the "appropriate government authorities." (See Chapter 16 for details about the establishment of the commission.)

Establishing internal investigation policy and resources that will uncover illegal violations is one of the few ways organizations can reduce their liability under government regulations, the Sentencing Commission's Guidelines, and possibly avoid costly litigation. Responding too quickly to a suspected offense, gathering evidence, and punishing personnel swiftly and drastically could be a fatal error.

Everyone involved in an internal investigation must be aware of the organization's policy and strategy on internal investigations, the laws that could have been violated by the organization or its personnel, and laws affecting the gathering of information and evidence. Every organization should have an internal investigation "game plan." This means, first, a board of directors resolution or a policy directive from management that clarifies and answers the following questions:

- What misconduct (broadly defined and at what level) will trigger an internal investigation?
- To whom should the incident or misconduct be reported?
- When should an investigation be initiated?
- Who should conduct the internal investigation and under what circumstances?
- What should be the purpose of the investigation?
- What types of disclosures are mandatory?

Corporate management must take the lead for several reasons. First, there are legal disclosure and reporting requirements. Second, there are practical considerations; perhaps, a company has multiple divisions or offices scattered around the country where local management will have neither the experience nor the training to deal with a criminal incident. A reporting and investigation policy sets up a formal system for handling incidents as well as giving management another form of control over corporatewide activities.

Investigative methodology and techniques, legal restraints, and evidence gathering discussed in previous chapters can be applied to compliance investigations. The primary goal of a compliance investigation, however, is to provide legal guidance to the corporation regarding possible violations of law and to minimize the damage resulting from such violations.

The next several chapters outline the requirements for conducting prompt, efficient, and diligent internal compliance investigations as set forth in the U.S. Sentencing Commission's organizational guidelines, voluntary compliance programs, and reporting requirements in various statutes. The emphasis here is on the need for a practical, cost-effective investigative game plan—in methodology and techniques as well as in the selection of legal counsel, auditors, and investigators for the investigative team. And, properly prepared reports—to a board of directors, an audit committee, or management—should contain meaningful findings, early warnings of problems, and provide important recommendations for action. The vital issue of information access and control, including relevant legal aspects of privileges, discovery, evidence, search and seizure, disclosure requirements, and confidentiality, is examined along with critical laws and regulations (e.g., Racketeering Influenced and Corrupt Organizations Act, money laundering, forfeiture, and the Financial Crime Kingpin Statute).

15

Financial Crimes Law

This chapter reviews laws that cover fraud and financial reporting as well as three major statutes that have profoundly affected the prosecution of financial crime: the Racketeering Influenced and Corrupt Organizations (RICO) Act, money laundering, and forfeiture. Each of the laws just mentioned are relatively recent, as far as either creation or implementation, and each has been used for purposes far beyond its supposedly original intention. Along with the U.S. Sentencing Commission's Guidelines, the laws have become the most potent weapons in the prosecutor's legal arsenal.

The RICO Act was originally designed to combat organized crime and get at individuals and organizations running criminal enterprises. The money laundering statutes were devised primarily to surveil and seize the proceeds from the drug trade and banks that were used in the laundering of money from drugs.

The forfeiture-of-property statute goes back to the "takings" clause of the Constitution; however, today forfeiture clauses have been inserted into virtually every criminal statute and many civil laws as well. Forfeiture has been used to seize assets of individuals prior to trial, thus disabling an effective defense.

A new law, the Financial Crime Kingpin Statute, has all the potential for becoming a strategic weapon for the prosecutor—the statute is vague, can be applied to an individual or a group, and has draconian penalties. In addition, like the rest of the statutes discussed, it can be used by the prosecution to threaten, intimidate, wring concessions, force cooperation, or compel plea bargaining from defendants.

FOREIGN CORRUPT PRACTICES ACT
Accounting Controls and the Act

The investigations of the Watergate special prosecutor and the Watergate Committee turned up a number of cases of questionable and illegal payments and contributions to the Nixon reelection campaign. Probing deeper and wider, the investigations uncovered corporate domestic political payments, as well as a pattern of payoffs and bribes to officials, functionaries, and business agents in foreign countries. These latter payments were either bribes or the common "grease" to ensure that operations went quickly and smoothly in the foreign business environment. As anyone who has ever traveled outside the United States knows, these practices were not, and are not, uncommon.

Congress, sensing public disapproval of these practices, sought to put a stop to future bribery and payoffs to foreign officials by enacting the Foreign Corrupt Practices Act (FCPA) (PL 95-213) in December 1977. In its antibribery section, the FCPA prohibits every U.S. business from certain corrupt practices in dealing with foreign officials. The act also amends the Securities and Exchange Act of 1934, which created the Securities and Exchange Commission (SEC), by imposing on companies registered with the SEC certain record-keeping and internal control standards designed to prevent companies from hiding foreign payments. The "accounting standards" provision of the act requires affected companies to:

a. Make and keep books, records, and accounts, which, in reasonable detail, accurately and fairly reflect the transactions and disposition of the assets of the issuer; and
b. Devise and maintain a system of internal accounting controls sufficient to provide reasonable assurance that 1) transactions are

executed in accordance with management's general or specific authorizations; 2) transactions are recorded as necessary to permit preparation of financial statements in conformity with generally accepted accounting principals or any other criteria applicable to such statements; 3) access to assets is permitted only in accordance with management's general or specific authorizations; and 4) the recorded accountability for assets is compared with the existing assets at reasonable intervals, and appropriate action is taken with respect to any difference.

An addition to the act, Rule 13(b)(2)-1, makes it illegal for any person to "directly or indirectly falsify or cause to be falsified any book, record or account," subject to section a. above. Another addition, Rule 13(b)(2)-2, makes it illegal for a director or officer of an affected company to directly or indirectly "make or cause to be made a materially false or misleading statement . . . or to omit to state a material fact" to an accountant during an audit or in preparing required SEC documents. In its release of these additions, the SEC said that

[T]hese rules, while intended to deal with a much broader range of practices than the problem of illegal corporate payments and practices, will serve to discourage repetition of the serious abuses which the Commission has uncovered in this area. The Commission's experience indicates that improper corporate payments and practices are rarely reflected in corporate books, records and accounts in an accurate manner and that the desire to conceal information concerning such activities frequently entails the falsification of books, records, and accounts and the making of false, misleading or incomplete statements to accountants.

There has been a good deal of dissent on the applicability of to "falsify"; that is, the phrase did not set a clear standard of wrongful intent for culpable conduct. An act of falsification should be intentional and any attempt to circumvent a control system should be deliberate under Rule 13(b)(2)-1.

FCPA Amendments The Omnibus Trade and Competitiveness Act of 1988 (PL 100-418) amends the FCPA by:

1. Defining the level of culpability as "knowing"—that the person either knows, or has a firm belief, that someone is engag-

ing in misconduct, that the circumstances exist, or that such result is substantially certain to occur. The prosecution must prove beyond a reasonable doubt that the defendant meets this requisite state of mind.

2. Adopting a standard of reasonableness—"a level of detail and degree of assurance as would satisfy prudent officials" that accounting controls and records are adequately maintained.

A criminal violation occurs when someone knowingly falsifies accounting records, circumvents, or fails to implement an internal accounting control system.

Conclusion The law's broadest powers have nothing to do with its stated chief intent—curbing bribery of and payoffs to foreign officials. The law can and has been used for domestic as well as foreign cases. The most significant provisions of the FCPA, therefore, are the "accounting standards," which make it a criminal offense for SEC-registered companies not to maintain accurate books and records and systems of internal controls.

Bribery Provisions of FCPA

In 1977, the FCPA amended the Securities and Exchange Act of 1934, Section 103(a), by inserting the following after Section 30:

> **Persons Covered:** (A) It shall be unlawful for any issuer which has a class of securities registered pursuant to section 12 of this title or which is required to file reports under section 15(d) of this title, or for any officer, director, employee, or agent of such issuer or any stockholder thereof acting on behalf of such issuer, to make use of the mails or any means or instrumentality of interstate commerce corruptly in furtherance of an offer, payment, promise to pay, or authorization of the payment of any money, or offer, gift, promise to give, or authorization of the giving of anything of value to—
>
> **Prohibited Acts and Receipts;**
> (1) Any foreign official for purposes of—
>   (A) influencing any act or decision of such foreign official in his [*sic*] official capacity, including a decision to fail to perform his official functions; or
>   (B) inducing such foreign official to use his influence with a foreign government or instrumentality thereof to

affect or influence any act or decision of such government or instrumentality, in order to assist such issuer in obtaining or retaining business for or with, or directing business to, any person;

(2) Any foreign political party or official thereof or any candidate for foreign political office for purposes of—

   (A) influencing any act or decision of such party, official, or candidate in its or his official capacity, including a decision to fail to perform his official functions; or

   (B) inducing such party, official, or candidate to use its or his influence with a foreign government or instrumentality thereof to affect or influence any act or decision of such government or instrumentality, in order to assist such issuer in obtaining or retaining business for or with, or directing business to, any person; or

(3) any person, while knowing or having reason to know that all or a portion of such money or thing of value will be offered, given, or promised, directly or indirectly, to any foreign official, to any foreign political party or official thereof, or to any candidate for foreign political office, for purposes of—

   (A) influencing any act or decision of such foreign official, political party, party official, or candidate in his or its official capacity, including a decision to fail to perform his or its official functions; or

   (B) inducing such foreign official, political party, party official, or candidate to use his or its influence with a foreign government or instrumentality thereof to affect or influence any act or decision of such government or instrumentality, in order to assist such issuer in obtaining or retaining business for or with, or directing business to, any person.

Definition of the Term "Foreign Official"   (b) As used in this section, the term "foreign official" means any officer or employee of a foreign government or any department, agency, or instrumentality thereof, or any person acting in an official capacity for or on behalf of such government or department, agency, or instrumentality. Such term does not include any employee of a foreign government or any department, agency, or instrumentality thereof whose duties are essentially ministerial or clerical.

Penalties
(b) (1) Section 32(a) of the Securities and Exchange Act of 1934 (15 U.S.C. 78ff(a)) is amended by inserting "(other than section 30A)" immediately after "title" the first place it appears. (2) Section 32 of the Securities and Exchange

Act of 1934 (15 U.S.C. 78ff) is amended by adding at the end thereof the following new subsection:

(c) (1) Any issuer who violates section 30A(a) of this title shall, upon conviction, be fined not more than $1,000,000.

(2) Any officer or director of an issuer, or any stockholder acting on behalf of such issuer, who willfully violates section 30A(a) of this title shall, upon conviction, be fined not more than $10,000, or imprisoned not more than five years, or both.

(3) Whenever an issuer is found to have violated section 30A(a) of this title, any employee or agent of such issuer who is a United States citizen, national or resident or is otherwise subject to the jurisdiction of the United States (other than an officer, director, or shareholder of such issuer), and who willfully carried out the act or practice constituting such violation shall, upon conviction, by fined not more than $10,000, or imprisoned not more than five years, or both.

(4) Whenever a fine is imposed under paragraph (2) or (3) of this subsection upon any officer, director, stockholder, employee, or agent of an issuer, such fine shall not be paid, directly or indirectly, by such issuer."

Domestic Concerns

Section 104 imposes the same above restrictions and penalties on domestics concerns, which are defined as:

a. Any individual who is a citizen, national, or resident of the United States.

b. Any corporation, partnership, association, joint-stock company, business trust, unincorporated organization or sole proprietorship which has its principal place of business in the United States, or which is organized under the laws of a state of the United States or a territory, possession, or commonwealth of the United States.

SECURITIES STATUTES

The key statutes and sections that outline elements of securities fraud follow. The first is the Securities Act of 1933 (15 U.S.C., Sections 77a–77mm); Section 77q(a) (1988) provides:

It shall be unlawful for any person in the offer or sale of any securities by the use of any means or instruments of transportation or communication in interstate commerce or by the use of the mails, directly or indirectly—
(1) to employ any device, scheme, or artifice to defraud, or
(2) to obtain money or property by means of any untrue statement of a material fact or any omission to state a material fact necessary in order to make the statements made, in the light of the circumstances under which they were made, not misleading, or
(3) to engage in any transaction, practice, or course of business which operates or would operate as a fraud or deceit upon the purchaser.

The Securities Exchange Act of 1934 (15 U.S.C., Sections 78a–78ll); Section 10(b) provides:

It shall be unlawful for any person, directly or indirectly, by the use of any means or instrumentality of interstate commerce or of the mails, or of any facility of any national securities exchange . . .
(b) to use or employ, in connection with the purchase or sale of any security registered on a national securities exchange or any security not so registered, any manipulative or deceptive device or contrivance in contravention of such rules and regulations as the Commission may prescribe as necessary or appropriate in the public interest or for the protection of investors.

Rule 10(b)-5 under the 1934 act provides:

It shall be unlawful for any person, directly or indirectly, by the use of any means or instrumentality of interstate commerce, or of the mails or of any facility of any national securities exchange—
(a) to employ any device, scheme, or artifice to defraud;
(b) to make any untrue statement of material fact or to omit to state a material fact necessary in order to make the statements made, in the light of the circumstances under which they were made, not misleading; or
(c) to engage in any act, practice, or course of business which operates or would operate as a fraud or deceit upon any person, in connection with the purchase or sale of any security.

Three elements are needed to prove securities fraud:

1. A substantive fraud exists, including material misrepresentations or omissions, a scheme or artifice to defraud, or a fraudulent act, practice or course of business;
2. Fraud must be connected to the sale or purchase of a security or in the offer or sale of a security; and
3. The fraud must use the mails or interstate commerce.

The elements of liability under the 1934 Act are:

1. The defendant committed a misstatement or omission of a material fact;
2. Made with scienter [intent, shown by a motive for and clear opportunity to commit fraud];
3. The plaintiff reasonably relied on the misstatement or omission of a material fact;
4. The misstatement or omission was a proximate cause of injury to the plaintiff.

The information is material if there is "a substantial likelihood that the disclosure of the omitted fact would have been viewed by the reasonable investor as having significantly altered the `total mix' of information made available" (Rule 100-5).

FEDERAL CRIMINAL STATUTES AND FINANCIAL CRIME

The following federal criminal statutes are commonly violated in crimes against financial institutions:

18 U.S.C. 215—kickbacks and bribes prohibition: making it unlawful for any officer, director, employee, agent, et al. (hereafter "insiders") of a financial institution to solicit, accept, or give anything of value in connection with a transaction or the business of the institution. (This statute was enacted in 1984.)

18 U.S.C. 641—larceny, embezzlement, or conversion of public monies or property of the United States.

18 U.S.C. 656—theft, embezzlement, or misapplication of the bank's money, funds, or credit willfully by an [officer, employee, or others connected to] with intent to injure or defraud a national bank, fed-

erally insured bank or branch or agency of a foreign bank. (Section 657 covers lending, credit, and insurance institutions.)

18 U.S.C. 1344—financial institution fraud: scheme or artifice to defraud a federally insured institution to take money, funds, credits, assets, securities, or other property by misrepresentation. (This statute was enacted in 1984.)

18 U.S.C. 1001—general false statements statute: knowingly and willfully falsifying or concealing a material fact or making a false statement, etc.

18 U.S.C. 1005—false entries in bank documents including material omissions, with intent to injure or defraud the commercial bank regulatory agencies' examiners or other individuals or companies.

18 U.S.C. 1014—false statement (oral or written), such as a loan application, an agreement with the financial institution or another document, made knowingly for the purpose of influencing any federally insured institutions (which would include an intentional overvaluing of real estate).

18 U.S.C. 1341 and 1343—mail and wire fraud, respectively: a scheme or artifice to defraud that makes use of either the U.S. mail or electrical transmission (including telephones).

18 U.S.C. 2 and 371—the general federal aiding and abetting statute and the general federal conspiracy statute, often applicable when two or more persons are involved in the commission of an offense.

Bank Fraud

The statute contained in 18 U.S.C. 1344 reads as follows:

> (a) Whoever knowingly executes, or attempts to execute, a scheme or artifice—
> (1) to defraud a financial institution; or
> (2) to obtain any of the moneys, funds, credits, assets, securities or other property owned by or under the custody or control of a financial institution by means of false or fraudulent pretenses, representations, or promises, shall be fined not more than $1,000,000, or imprisoned not more than 30 years, or both.

Under the Crime Control Act of 1990, Congress lengthened the statute of limitations for bank fraud to ten years.

White-Collar Crime Kingpin Statute

Also enacted under the Crime Control Act of 1990, Section 2510, was the Financial Crime Kingpin Statute—the only fraud statute that carries a mandatory minimum sentence. The act amends the Continuing Financial Crimes Enterprises (18 U.S.C., Section 225) by providing:

> (a) Whoever—
> > (1) organizes, manages, or supervises a continuing financial crimes enterprise; and
> > (2) receives $5,000,000 or more in gross receipts from such enterprise during any 24-month period, shall be fined not more than $10,000,000 if an individual, or $20,000,000 if an organization, and imprisoned for a term of not less than 10 years and which may be life.
> (b) For purposes of subsection (a), the term `continuing financial crimes enterprise' means a series of violations under 215, 656, 657, 1005, 1006, 1007, 1014, 1032, or 1344 of this title, or section 1342 or 1343 affecting a financial institution, committed by at least 4 persons acting in concert.

Bank Bribery Amendments

The Bank Bribery Amendments Act of 1985 (18 U.S.C. 215) covers the receipt of commissions or gifts for procuring loans, specifically:

> (a) Whoever—
> > (1) corruptly gives, offers, or promises anything of value to any person, with intent to influence or reward an officer, director, employee, agent, or attorney of a financial institution in connection with any business or transaction of such institution; or
> > (2) as an officer, director, employee, agent, or attorney of a financial institution, corruptly solicits or demands for the benefit of any person, or corruptly accepts or agrees to accept, anything of value from any person, intending to be influenced or rewarded in connection with any business or transaction of such institution; shall be fined not more than $5,000 or three times the value of the thing given, offered, promised, solicited, demanded, accepted, or agreed to be accepted, whichever is greater, or imprisoned not more than five years, or both, but if the value of the thing given, offered, promised, solicited, demanded, accepted, or agreed

to be accepted does not exceed $100, shall be fined not more than $1,000 or imprisoned not more than one year, or both.

Commercial Bribery

Compromising the decision or judgment of someone who has a legal, moral, or fiduciary duty to remain faithful and free of corruption is called *bribery*. Generally, bribery comes in two forms: political and commercial. Political bribery has been with mankind since the dawn of recorded history. Commercial bribery is of a more recent vintage. It came about as a side effect of the Industrial Revolution and the large-scale production of goods and services.

In the typical commercial bribery situation, an outside vendor, supplier, or contractor curries favor with an inside person who has authority to make or recommend a purchase decision, by offering or giving something of value to that person. Under these circumstances, both the payor and payee have a reason to conceal the transaction: the giver because such a payment may be a crime and is not tax deductible; the recipient because such receipt may be a crime and may constitute taxable income. In each case of bribery, accordingly, there is a likelihood of other crimes such as false statements, false entries, and tax evasion. The concealment efforts are intended to disguise the true nature of the payment and the identities of the recipient and payor of the bribe.

Commercial bribery takes many disguised forms (e.g., the giving and accepting of cash, property, or privilege under the guise of a fee, wage, commission, charitable contribution, free sample, gift, gratuity, entertainment, loan, debt payment, free use of a vehicle, vacation home, or free travel, token of remembrance, or procurement of "evening companions"). The essence of commercial bribery is that a victimized firm is paying more than fair market value for the products and services it requires, or getting inferior quality and untimely performance.

Under New York state law, commercial bribery occurs when a person "confers, offers or agrees to confer any benefit upon an employee, agent or fiduciary without the consent of the latter's employer or principal, with intent to influence his [*sic*] conduct in relation to his employer's or principal's affairs." The statute also makes an employee or agent guilty of bribery if he or she solicits or agrees to accept any gratuity or benefit. Bribery under the New York statute is a misdemeanor if the bribe is worth more than $1,000. While nearly half of the states have statutes proscribing commercial bribery, the violation is usually a misdemeanor.

Investigating and Proving Bribery   Proving bribery in a criminal case is no mean task, given the concealment options available to the bribe giver and bribe taker. Both are inclined to seal their lips. So, how does one go about testing for and proving bribery? There are several audit and investigative steps in the case of a company that is victimized:

1. Analyze expense categories that are running higher than (a) expectations, (b) cost assumptions, and (c) long-term trends; then review the documentation that supports these expenditures for evidence of contrivance.
2. Check for previous allegations or complaints of payment or receipt of bribes involving the purchasing official and vendor.
3. Check for evidence of high living by the alleged bribe receiver.
4. Seek out other vendors whose bids to the company have been consistently rejected even though their prices and performance appear to be competitive and comparable.
5. Check for vendors whose price, quality, and performance records are consistently below standard and yet continue to get business from the firm.

Program Fraud and Bribery   Theft or bribery rules concerning programs receiving federal funds were amended in 1984 (18 U.S.C. 31) as follows:

(a) Whoever, being an agent of an organization, or of a state or local government agency, that receives benefits in excess of $10,000 in any one-year period pursuant to a federal program involving a grant, a contract, a subsidy, a loan, a guarantee, insurance, or another form of federal assistance, embezzles, steals, purloins, willfully misapplies, obtains by fraud, or otherwise knowingly without authority converts to his [*sic*] own use or to the use of another, property having a value of $5,000 or more owned by or under the care, custody, or control of such organization or state or local government agency, shall be imprisoned for not more than ten years and fined not more than $100,000 or an amount equal to twice that which was obtained in violation of this subsection, whichever is greater, or both so imprisoned and fined.

(b) Whoever, being an agent of an organization, or of a state or local government agency, described in subsection (a), solicits, demands, accepts, or agrees to accept anything of value from a person or organization other than his employer or principal for or because of the recipient's conduct in any transaction or matter or a series of transactions or matters involving $5,000 or more concerning the affairs of such organization or state or local government agency, shall be imprisoned for not more than ten years or fined not more than $100,000 or an amount equal to twice that which was obtained, demanded, solicited or agreed upon in violation of this subsection, whichever is greater, or both so imprisoned and fined.

(c) Whoever offers, gives, or agrees to give to an agent of an organization or of a state or local government agency, described in subsection (a), anything of value for or because of the recipient's conduct in any transaction or matter or any series of transactions or matters involving $5,000 or more concerning the affairs of such organization or state or local government agency, shall be imprisoned not more than ten years or fined not more than $100,000 or an amount equal to twice that offered, given or agreed to be given, whichever is greater, or both so imprisoned and fined.

Anti-Kickback Act

The Anti-Kickback Enforcement Act of 1986 amends Section 2(a) of the 1946 act (41 U.S.C. 51–54), which sought to

> eliminate the practice by subcontractors, under cost-plus-a-fixed-fee or cost reimbursable contracts of the United States, of paying fees or kickbacks, or of granting gifts or gratuities to employees of a cost-plus-fixed-fee or cost reimbursable prime contractors or of higher tier subcontractors for the purpose of securing the award of subcontracts or orders. . . .

Prohibited Conduct   Under Section 3(a), it is prohibited for any person—

(1) to provide, attempt to provide, or offer to provide any kickback;
(2) to solicit, accept, or attempt to accept any kickback; or

(3) to include, directly or indirectly, the amount of any kickback prohibited by clause (1) or (2) in the contract price charged by a subcontractor or in the contract price charged by a prime contractor to the United States.

Criminal Penalties   Section 4—Any person who knowingly and willfully engages in conduct prohibited by Section 3 shall be imprisoned for not more than ten years or shall be subject to a fine in accordance with Title 18 of the U.S. Code, or both.

Civil Actions   Under Section 5(a)(1) of the U.S. Code, the United States may, in a civil action, recover a civil penalty from any person who knowingly engages in conduct prohibited by Section 3.

The amount of such civil penalty shall be—
(a) twice the amount of each kickback involved in the violation; and
(b) not more than $10,000 for each occurrence of prohibited conduct . . .
(2) The United States may, in a civil action, recover a civil penalty from any person whose employee, subcontractor or subcontractor employee violates section 3 by providing, accepting, or charging a kickback. The amount of such civil penalty shall be the amount of that kickback.

CONSPIRACY LAWS

Conspiracy law is relevant to a discussion of crime, investigation, and litigation because conspiracy violations are often the first thing prosecutors look for as it is generally easier to obtain convictions under these statutes. The conspiracy statutes have been used in such a wide range of cases, limited, it seems, only by the imaginations of prosecutors and litigators. In dealing with a possible computer crime, however, it is wise to be practical and precise, rather than imaginative.

This discussion will cover the general conspiracy statutes, the Racketeer Influenced and Corrupt Organizations (RICO) law, and the statutes of mail and wire fraud, the two statutes commonly merged with or underlying conspiracy. In addition, we will show how these laws can be applied to fraud-related criminal and civil charges and used to facilitate recovery for damages.

Conspiracy

The general federal conspiracy statute, 18 U.S.C. 371, says

> If two or more persons conspire either to commit any offense against the United States, or to defraud the United States, or any agency thereof in any manner or for any purpose, and one or more of such persons do any act to effect the object of the conspiracy, each shall be fined not more than $10,000 or imprisoned not more than five years or both.

Conspiracy is a group crime, a group agreement, a deliberate plotting to subvert the law. The elements of the crime are: (a) the knowing and willful agreement to commit a crime, (b) between two or more persons, and (c) an action to carry out the conspiracy. Note that the crime of conspiracy is the agreement; this is the critical element.

Parties to such illegitimate agreements need not strike a bargain in the traditional business sense—create a written contract, agreement, memo, or have a meeting—to be prosecuted under the statute. It need only be shown that a person was: a party to a conspiratorial agreement to do something unlawful, during the existence of the conspiracy, that he or she knew what was involved, and was committed to taking part in it to ensure its success.

A person involved in a conspiracy is responsible for: all that happened during the conspiracy which he or she agreed to; that is, the acts of each of the confederates even though he or she may be unaware of each other's actions. A member of a conspiracy may get out or withdraw only by doing something to disavow or defeat the purpose of the conspiracy. However, he or she will remain liable for anything that happened prior to his or her withdrawal.

Evidence   It must be demonstrated that a person had knowledge of the conspiracy, that he or she agreed to it, and performed some act to further the conspiracy. Statements and acts of co-conspirators are admissible as evidence if they indicate the above.

Prosecution   To prosecute conspiracy, the offense must be within the court's venue. Usually conspiracy is merged with another crime because it is normally discovered after a crime has been committed.

Therefore, the charges are conspiracy plus a crime. In common law, and some state statutes, the charges are merged. The prosecution must also determine if there is was a single conspiracy or multiple conspiracies. A single conspiracy is a single agreement, although it may involve many persons, be complex, and continue over a long period of time.

Prosecutors are aware of the advantages of charging the conspiracy offense, which include the ease of joining charges, the admissibility of co-conspirators' statements, and that it is not necessary to show that each defendant actually committed the offense—only that he or she agreed to do so.

Summary   The act of conspiracy consists of the following:

- Two or more persons must agree to commit a criminal act;
- The agreement need only be inferred;
- At least one party to the conspiracy must perform some act in furtherance of the conspiracy (this act need not be criminal);
- One party may be held responsible for the acts of co-conspirators even though he or she did not commit any substantive offenses or have actual knowledge of them—a partnership in crime includes all members within its scope and during its time of operation;
- The agreement must be to either violate a criminal statute or, under federal law, to defraud the U.S. government. The definition of fraud is not limited to that of common law; the federal statute includes every conspiracy to impair, obstruct, or defeat any lawful function of the government.

Criminal Statutes Often Merge with Conspiracy

Mail Fraud   The mail fraud statute (18 U.S.C. 1341) provides:

> Whoever, having devised or intending to devise any scheme or artifice to defraud, or for obtaining money or property by means of false or fraudulent pretenses, representations, or promises, or to sell, dispose of, loan, exchange, alter, give away, distribute, supply, or furnish or procure for unlawful use any counterfeit or spurious coin, obligation, security, or other article, or anything represented to be or inti-

mated or held out to be such counterfeit or spurious article, for the purpose of executing such scheme or artifice or attempting to do so, places in any post office or authorized depository for mail matter, any matter or thing whatever to be sent or delivered by the Postal Service or takes or receives therefrom, any such matter or thing, or knowingly causes to be delivered by mail according to the direction thereon, or at the place at which it is directed to be delivered by the person to whom it is addressed, any such matter or thing, shall be fined not more than $1,000 or imprisoned not more than five years, or both.

Wire Fraud The essential elements of wire fraud (18 U.S.C. 1343) are: (1) the devising of a scheme and artifice to defraud; and (2) a transmittal in interstate or foreign commerce by means of wire, radio, or television communication of writings, signs, signals, pictures, or sounds for the purpose of executing the scheme and artifice to defraud. Here is where transmission of computer data over telephone lines fits. The statute provides:

> Whoever, having devised or intending to devise any scheme or artifice to defraud, or for obtaining money or property by means of false or fraudulent pretenses, representations or promises, transmits or causes to be transmitted by means of wire, radio, or television communication in interstate or foreign commerce, any writings, signs, signals, pictures, or sounds for the purpose of executing such scheme or artifice, shall be fined not more than $1,000 or imprisoned not more than five years, or both.

THE FEDERAL ANTI-RACKETEERING LAW

The federal anti-racketeering law, better known as the RICO Act (18 U.S.C., Sections 1961 to 1968), has become one of the main legal weapons against a host of crimes. However, its widespread use by prosecutors has caused private-sector opposition to RICO, claiming the law is being used indiscriminately, harshly, and in ways not originally intended. It has been argued that RICO was to apply to criminals and racketeers—as its title says—not for civil suits against corporations with no criminal record. Specifically, the law's treble damages award was seen as too severe for most civil cases.

Attempts to get the courts to change RICO received a critical setback in 1985 when the U.S. Supreme Court, in *American National*

Bank and Trust Co. of Chicago v. Haroco Inc., said that it was up to Congress to correct any problems with RICO. Opposition attempts therefore shifted to Congress.

In 1989, and in the next several years, Congress tried to change those provisions of RICO dealing with damage awards and criminal convictions and to restrict the use of RICO in civil suits. These reform proposals sought to drop treble damages and legal fees from most future RICO civil suits brought by private plaintiffs, to modify the forfeiture provisions, and to provide for "gatekeepers" to screen out frivolous or inappropriate lawsuits.

Prosecution Targets

The federal and state RICO statutes were originally intended to give the government a legal tool to use in prosecuting organized crime. Since it was passed in 1970, however, RICO has been used to prosecute Mafia figures, members of the Hells Angels motorcycle club, a former governor, commodity futures traders, securities brokers and firms, and antiabortion protestors.

Key Provisions of the RICO Statutes

RICO does have important application to fraud and computer crime cases, and to understand the statutes, one must be cognizant of several key phrases and terms:

> *Enterprise*—Section 1961(4) defines this as any individual, partnership, corporation, association, or other legal entity, any union or group of individuals associated in fact although not a legal entity.
>
> *Pattern of Racketeering Activity*—Encompasses both the act and the pattern of racketeering. The act of racketeering is defined by those statutes, state and federal, that are mostly broken in organized crime activity; the statute enumerates thirty-two such offenses. Included under state law are arson, bribery, extortion, dealing in narcotics or dangerous drugs, gambling, kidnapping, murder, and robbery.

Under Title 18 of the U.S. Code are these sections: 201 (bribery), 224 (sports bribery), 471–473 (counterfeiting), 659 (theft from interstate shipment), 664 (embezzlement from pension and welfare funds), 891–894 (extortionate credit transactions), 1084 (transmission of gambling information), 1341 (mail fraud), 1343 (wire fraud), 1503 (obstruction of justice), 1510 (obstruction of criminal investigations), 1511 (obstruction of state or local law enforcement), 1951 (interference with commerce, robbery, or extortion), 1952 (racketeering), 1953 (transportation of wagering paraphernalia), 1954 (unlawful welfare fund payments), 1955 (prohibition of illegal gambling businesses), 2314–2315 (interstate transportation of stolen property), and 2421–2424 (white slave traffic).

Under Title 29 of the U.S. Code are sections: 186 (restrictions on payments and loans to labor organizations) and 501(c) (embezzlement from union funds). Also included are offenses punishable under any U.S. law involving bankruptcy fraud, felonious manufacture or other dealing in narcotic or dangerous drugs, or securities fraud.

Under the Financial Institutions Reform, Recovery and Enforcement Act of 1989 (PL 101-73), RICO is applied to bank fraud. Environmental crimes and crimes against federal interest computers are now also under RICO.

Convictions Under RICO

At least two of the acts of racketeering described here must have a nexus, or connection (to form a pattern), with the enterprise itself. Thus, for the government to convict under RICO, it must prove both the existence of an enterprise and the connected pattern of racketeering activity. Of the two acts of racketeering, the most recent must have occurred within five years of the indictment, and another within ten years of the most recent act.

Penalties Under RICO

RICO provides both criminal penalties and civil remedies. Criminal penalties are twenty years imprisonment, a $25,000 fine, and forfeiture to the government of any interest in, or property in contractual right to, any enterprise acquired in violation of Section 1962. Civil remedies in RICO are similar to antitrust law; in addition, any person injured by the enterprise may sue and recover three times the damage sustained, plus court costs and reasonable attorney's fees.

Overview of Civil RICO Provisions

Civil RICO provisions (18 U.S.C., Sections 1964–1968) are predicated on the general RICO provisions in 18 U.S.C., Sections 1961 and 1962. A civil suit under RICO may be brought either by governments or by private persons. Civil RICO offers expansive remedies, including treble damages, the costs of investigations and prosecution, attorney's fees, and equitable relief.

Section 1964(a) gives federal district courts jurisdiction to grant injunctive and other equitable relief to prevent and restrain violations of Section 1962. Section 1964(a) authorizes courts to provide such relief by issuing appropriate orders, including, but not limited to:

1. Ordering any person to divest himself or herself of any interest in an enterprise;
2. Imposing reasonable restrictions on future activities or investments of any person, including prohibiting the person from engaging in the same kind of endeavor as the enterprise engaged in; and
3. Ordering dissolution or reorganization of any enterprise.

Section 1964(c) provides that "[a]ny person injured in his [sic] business or property by reason of a violation of Section 1962" may sue and recover treble damages, costs, and reasonable attorney's fees.

Section 1964(d) provides that a final judgment or decree rendered in favor of the United States in any criminal RICO proceeding estops the defendant from denying the essential allegations of the criminal offense in a subsequent civil RICO case brought by the government. This provision is very useful to the government when civil RICO cases are filed following a criminal prosecution. Basically, this provision prevents a defendant from contesting any of the factual allegations that were proved in the criminal proceeding. As a result, if the civil RICO suit is based on essentially the same allegations as the criminal RICO prosecution, the government should prevail on a motion for summary judgment against any defendants who were convicted in the criminal proceeding.

Sections 1965 through 1968 contain provisions involving procedural aspects of civil RICO actions—venue and service of process. Section 1966 provides for expedited treatment of civil RICO lawsuits brought by the government if the attorney general files with the court a certificate stating that the case is of public importance. Section 1967 provides that proceedings in or ancillary to civil RICO suits brought by the United States may be open or closed to the public "at the discretion of the court after consideration of the rights of affected persons." Section 1968, provides detailed procedures for the issuance of civil investigative demands by the United States prior to the institution of criminal or civil proceedings.

Cases and Court Decisions

In its criminal context, RICO has been upheld by the Supreme Court (see *Russello v. United States*), and cases that have been successfully prosecuted include arson, extortion, mail fraud, racketeering, and conspiracies to commit such crimes. And, the U.S. Supreme Court let stand a ruling by the 7th Circuit Court of Appeals (in *Schact v. Brown*) that indicates upholding of the civil side of RICO. The Court said such suits could go forward even if the defendant had not previously been convicted of a "mobster-type crime."

In *National Organization for Women, Inc., etc., et al. v. Joseph Scheidler et al.*, the Supreme Court accepted a writ of *certiorari* brought by petitioners, the National Organization for Women, Inc., and two health-care centers that perform abortions. In the suit, the respondents were a coalition of antiabortion groups called the Pro-Life Action Network (PLAN) and others. The petitioners sued alleging violations of the RICO statute; an amended complaint added violations of the Hobbs Act. The petitioners claimed that respondents were members of a nationwide conspiracy to shut down abortion clinics through a pattern of racketeering activity, including extortion. The proabortion groups sought injunctive relief, along with treble damages, costs, and attorney's fees.

Both the federal district court and the court of appeals had dismissed the case. These courts said that the voluntary contributions received by the anti-abortion groups did not constitute income derived from racketeering activities for puposes of RICO. They also said that noneconomic crimes that are committed in furtherance of some noneconomic motive are not within the ambit of RICO.

The Supreme Court took the case to resolve a conflict among the courts on the putative economic motive requirement of specific RICO provisions—1962(c) and (d); that is, whether the racketeering enterprise or the racketeering predicate acts must be accompanied by an underlying economic motive. Nowhere in the act's definitions did the Supreme Court find any indication that an economic motive is required. Subsection 1962(c) may suggest that there be a profit-seeking motive, but in *NOW v. Schiedler* the Court argued that "enterprise" in this subsection

> connotes generally the vehicle through which the unlawful pattern of racketeering activity is committed, rather than the victim of that activity. . . . Consequently, since the enterprise in subsection (c) is not being acquired, it need not have a property interest that can be acquired nor an economic motive for engaging in illegal activity; it need only be an association in fact that engages in a pattern of racketeering activity. Nothing in subsections (a) and (b) directs us to a contrary conclusion.

Nor do predicate acts require an underlying economic motive. Predicate acts, such as an alleged extortion, may not benefit people financially, but they still drain money from the economy by harming businesses. The Court thought the requirement of an economic motive was neither expressed nor that it was fairly implied in the operative sections of the act.

State RICO Statutes

State RICO statutes often give prosecutors authority to sue on behalf of the state and its citizens who suffer a "business or property" injury. Most states have designed their civil RICO statutes based on the federal RICO. Typical state statutes prohibit: (1) investing the proceeds of a "pattern of racketeering activity" in an enterprise; (2) taking control of an enterprise through a pattern of racketeering; (3) infiltrating an enterprise and engaging in a pattern of racketeering through it; and (4) conspiring to do any of the others here. State statutes may substitute the term "criminal profiteering activity" for "racketeering activity." The underlying offenses (racketeering acts) may be a wide selection of state and federal crimes.

Again, the key phrases to examine in state RICO statutes are "pattern" and "enterprise," to see how precisely they are defined. Legal remedies usually include treble damages, attorney's fees and costs, civil forfeiture, and civil penalties.

As of this writing, the states and territories with RICO statutes are: Arizona, California, Colorado, Connecticut, Delaware, Florida, Georgia, Hawaii, Idaho, Illinois, Indiana, Louisiana, Minnesota, Mississippi, Nevada, New Jersey, New Mexico, New York, North Carolina, North Dakota, Ohio, Oklahoma, Oregon, Pennsylvania, Rhode Island, Tennessee, Utah, Washington, Wisconsin, Puerto Rico, and the Virgin Islands.

Arguments for Limiting RICO

As stated earlier, whether the use of RICO will expand further into the civil area, or be limited to specific criminal acts committed by organized criminals, remains to be decided by Congress and the courts. Congress has sought to eliminate the civil treble-damage award unless the defendant had a prior criminal conviction. Victims who could prove they were victims of a pattern of criminal or fraudulent conduct and that the defendant acted in "wanton disregard" of their rights could collect double-damage awards. Recent reform legislation, which did not pass Congress, would have reserved civil RICO remedies for cases brought from "egregious criminal conduct." And, judges could be "gatekeepers," keeping out suits that did not meet the egregious standard.

Congressional reformers have argued that the current misuse of civil RICO is hampering its original purpose, which was meant to be "an extraordinary Federal remedy for particularly offensive activities that harmed all of society" (U.S. Senate Report 101-269, p. 2, April 24, 1990). Meanwhile, the courts have taken up the task of clarifying sections of RICO. In the 1992 case of *Holmes v. Securities Investor Protection Corp.*, the Supreme Court made it harder to file lawsuits under civil RICO by ruling that an injured plaintiff must show that the defendant's violation was the "proximate cause" of the injury suffered by the plaintiff. This case seems to establish a direct-harm test for all civil RICO plaintiffs.

In an appeal filed in the *Wedtech* case, former federal judge Robert Bork summarized typical legal objections to RICO:

> RICO is constitutionally intolerable. The Due Process Clause of the Fifth Amendment forbids Congress from enacting penal statutes that are so vague and indefinite as to deprive a person of ordinary

intelligence of notice of the prohibited conduct, and to afford unfettered discretion to prosecutors. . . . RICO grants essentially unbridled discretion to judges and juries. . . .

The key statutory elements—the existence of an "enterprise" and . . . "pattern of racketeering"—have no limiting definition in the statute. Nor does either of these statutory terms provide any notice of what is actually forbidden.

In a 1993 case, *Reves et al. v. Ernst & Young*, the Supreme Court further clarified RICO's operations or management test. The accounting firm of Ernst & Young was charged with securities fraud and RICO violations, that of overvaluing assets and thus helping to keep the farm co-op a going concern as well as a client. RICO makes it unlawful for anyone employed by or associated with an interstate enterprise to conduct or directly or indirectly participate in the conduct of an enterprise's affairs through a pattern of racketeering activity. The court ruled that the plaintiffs/shareholders did not prove that, for liability to attach, there must be some sort of participation in the operation or management of the actual enterprise.

The plaintiffs failed to show anything more than that Ernest & Young reviewed a series of completed transactions, and certified the co-op's records as portraying its financial status fairly. In defining the operations test in *Reves*, the Court said, "once it is understood that the word 'conduct' requires some degree of direction, and that the word 'participate' requires some part in that direction, it is clear that one must have some part in directing an enterprise's affairs in order to 'participate, directly or indirectly, in the conduct of such . . . affairs.'"

Action for clarifying, modifying, or limiting RICO will stay with the courts, especially the Supreme Court. The Court has even invited cases that would challenge specific provisions of RICO. There is no doubt, then, that RICO will face intense scrutiny as to its constitutionality by the Supreme Court.

Conclusion

RICO, criminal and civil, is a potent weapon in the prosecution's arsenal. RICO is a complex law with harsh criminal penalties and expansive civil remedies. It is also a law with provisions that could be clarified or limited by the higher courts. Conspiracy laws should be discussed with legal counsel at the outset of any fraud or computer fraud-related incident that might involve a violation of law. Issues of evidence gathering, discovery, merged or underlying offenses, or recovery of damages should all be thoroughly examined prior to an investigation or filing of legal charges.

MONEY LAUNDERING

The Money Laundering Control Act (18 U.S.C. 1956–1957) was passed in October 1986 as part of the Anti-Drug Abuse Act of 1986. The act created two new offenses related to money laundering and currency transaction reporting violations. Parties engaged in certain cash transactions are required to report the following:

    a. banks and financial institutions must report transactions of $10,000 or more in cash in a single transaction or related transactions;

    b. persons transporting monetary instruments into or out of the United States;

    c. financial institutions must verify the identity of persons who purchase bank checks, traveler's checks, or money orders in amounts of $3,000 or more;

    d. A Foreign Bank Account Report is required whenever a person has an account in a foreign bank of more than $5,000 in value.

Treasury regulations require a paper trail of bank records that must be maintained for up to five years.

Money laundering violations are now predicate acts under RICO. Title 18 of the U.S. Code, Section 1957, states:

    (a)(1) Whoever, knowing that the property involved in a financial transaction represents the proceeds of some form of unlawful activity, conducts or attempts to conduct such a financial transaction which in fact involves the proceeds of specified unlawful activity—

    (A) with the intent to promote the carrying on of specified unlawful activity; or

    (B) knowing that the transaction is designed in whole or in part—

      (i) to conceal or disguise the nature, the location, the source, the ownership, or the control of the proceeds of specified unlawful activity; or

(ii) to avoid a transaction reporting requirement under state or federal law, shall be sentenced to a fine of not more than $500,000 or twice the value of the property involved in the transaction, whichever is greater, or imprisonment for not more than twenty years, or both.

(2) Whoever transports or attempts to transport a monetary instrument or funds from a place in the United States to or through a place outside the United States or to a place in the United States from or through a place outside the United States—

(A) with the intent to promote the carrying on of specified unlawful activity; or

(B) knowing that the monetary instrument or funds involved in the transportation represent the proceeds of some form of unlawful activity and knowing that such transportation is designed in whole or in part—

(i) to conceal or disguise the nature, the location, the source, the ownership, or the control of the proceeds of specified unlawful activity; or

(ii) to avoid a transaction reporting requirement under state or federal law, shall be sentenced to a fine of $500,000 or twice the value of the monetary instrument or funds involved in the transportation, whichever is greater, or imprisonment for not more than twenty years, or both.

(b) Whoever conducts or attempts to conduct a transaction described in subsection (a)(1), or a transportation described in subsection (a)(2), is liable to the United States for a civil penalty of not more than the greater of—

(1) the value of the property, funds, or monetary instruments involved in the transaction; or

(2) $10,000.

When engaging in monetary transactions in property derived from specified unlawful activity, the Code states:

(a) Whoever, in any of the circumstances set forth in subsection (d), knowingly engages or attempts to engage in a monetary transaction in criminally derived property of a value greater than $10,000 and is derived from specified unlawful activity, shall be punished as provided in subsection (b).

(b) (1) Except as provided in paragraph (2), the punishment of an offense under this section is a fine under title 18,

U.S. Code, or imprisonment for not more than ten years, or both.

(2) The court may impose an alternate fine to that imposable under paragraph (1) of not more than twice the amount of the criminally derived property involved in the transaction.

FORFEITURE STATUTES

Forfeiture statutes are either criminal or civil in nature. A criminal forfeiture is litigated in the trial that determines the defendant's guilt and is ordered only after the defendant/violator is found guilty. Because other parties who may have an interest in the forfeitable property cannot participate in the criminal trial, a verdict of forfeiture settles title in favor of the government only as against the criminal defendant. Post-trial hearings must be held in order to allow third-party claimants to defend their interests in the property.

Conversely, a civil forfeiture is not an action against an individual but an action against the property itself. Civil forfeiture proceedings can be completed before a criminal defendant is charged or convicted, after the defendant's acquittal, or even absent any criminal charge. Unlike criminal forfeiture actions where the government must prove the forfeitable offense beyond a reasonable doubt, the burden of proof in civil forfeiture actions shifts to the claimant once the government has established probable cause to sustain the forfeiture. A civil forfeiture action settles the government's title to the property as against the world. No further proceedings relating to property title are necessary.

Some forfeiture statutes do not specify whether the mode of enforcement is a criminal or a civil action and the legislative history fails to resolve the issue. In such instances, 28 U.S.C., Section 2461, provides a strong argument that such statutes should be enforced through an *in rem* civil proceeding.

Fraud Laws with Forfeiture Provisions

Title 18, U.S.C. Section 981, Civil Forfeiture Relating to Money Laundering Offenses, and Title 18, U.S.C., Section 981, as added to by Section 1366(a) of the Anti-Drug Abuse Act of 1986 (PL 99-570) authorize civil forfeiture relating to money laundering. Subsection

981(a)(1), which describes three types of property forfeitable to the United States, provides as follows:

Section 981. Civil Forfeiture

(a)(1) Except as provided in paragraph (2), the following property is subject to forfeiture to the United States:

(A) Any property, real or personal, which represents the gross receipts a person obtains, directly or indirectly, as a result of a violation of section 1956 or 1957 of this title, or which is traceable to such gross receipts.

(B) Any property within the jurisdiction of the United States, which represents the proceeds of an offense against a foreign nation involving the manufacture, importation, sale, or distribution of a controlled substance (as such term is defined for the purposes of the Controlled Substances Act), within whose jurisdiction such offense or activity would be punishable by death or imprisonment for a term exceeding one year and which would be punishable by imprisonment for a term exceeding one year if such act or activity had occurred within the jurisdiction of the United States.

(C) Any coin and currency (or other monetary instrument as the Secretary of the Treasury may prescribe) or any interest in other property, including any deposit in a financial institution, traceable to such coin or currency involved in a transaction or attempted transaction in violation of section 5313(a) or 5324 of title 31 may be seized and forfeited to the United States Government. No property or interest in property shall be seized or forfeited if the violation is by a domestic financial institution examined by a Federal bank supervisory agency or a financial institution regulated by the Securities and Exchange Commission or a partner, director, officer, or employee thereof.

16

Sentencing Guidelines for Individuals

The sentencing guidelines for federal crimes have been prepared by the U.S. Sentencing Commission. The commission was established by the Sentencing Reform Act of 1984 and was charged with drafting guidelines for federal judges to use when sentencing convicted defendants. The objective of the act was an effective, fair sentencing system; Congress sought to obtain honesty, reasonable uniformity, and proportionality in sentencing. *Honesty* means the sentence imposed by the court is the sentence the offender will serve; abolishing parole was one method to this end. Narrowing the wide disparity in sentences imposed for similar criminal offenses committed by similar offenders is a way to achieve *reasonable uniformity*. Imposing appropriately different sentences for criminal conduct of differing severity achieves the objective of *proportionality* in sentencing.

The act directs the commission to create categories of offense behavior and offender characteristics. In 1986, the commission asked for and got legislation to deal with issuance of general policy statements concerning imposition of fines, the permissible width of a guideline range calling for a term of imprisonment, and appellate review of sentences. A federal court must select a sentence from within the guideline range. In an atypical case, the court is allowed a departure from the guideline, but must specify reasons for the departure; however, such a departure may be reviewed by an appellate court. The federal sentencing guidelines took effect on November 1, 1987.

THE SENTENCING TABLE AND INSTRUCTIONS

For technical and practical reasons, the commission has established a sentencing table that contains forty-three levels (see page 175). Each level in the table prescribes ranges that overlap with the ranges in the preceding and succeeding levels. In applying the guidelines, one must first determine the applicable offense guideline section. For example, for computer-related fraud, 18 U.S.C., Sections 1029 and 1030—Part F, Offenses Involving Fraud or Deceit (2F1.1).

The next step is to determine the base offense level and to apply any appropriate specific offense characteristics contained in the particular guideline. Each offense may cover one statute or many and has a corresponding base offense level and may have one or more specific characteristics that adjust the offense level upward or downward. Other instructions must be applied, depending on the particular offense and case.

The following discussion presents the guidelines for fraud, including computer-related fraud, with comments on sentencing-related cases and instructions. This guideline is designed to apply to a wide variety of fraud cases. The statutory maximum term of imprisonment for most such offenses is five years. The guideline does not link offense characteristics to specific code sections. Because federal fraud statutes are so broadly written, a single pattern of offense conduct usually can be prosecuted under several code sections, as a result of which the offense of conviction may be somewhat arbitrary. Furthermore, most fraud statutes cover a broad range of conduct with extreme variation in severity.

Empirical analyses of pre-guideline practices showed that the most important factors that determined sentence length were the amount of loss and whether the offense was an isolated crime of opportunity or was sophisticated or repeated. Accordingly, although they are imperfect, these are the primary factors on which the guideline has been based. The extent to which an offense is planned or sophisticated is important in assessing its potential harmfulness and the dangerousness of the offender, independent of actual harm. A complex scheme or repeated incidents of fraud are indicative of an intention and potential to do considerable harm.

In pre-guidelines practice, this factor had a significant impact, especially in frauds involving small losses. Accordingly, the guideline specifies a two-level enhancement when this factor is present. A defendant who has been subject to civil or administrative proceedings for the same or similar fraudulent conduct demonstrates aggravated criminal intent and is deserving of additional punishment for not conforming with the requirements of judicial process or orders issued by federal, state, or local administrative agencies.

Offenses that involve the use of transactions or accounts outside the United States in an effort to conceal illicit profits and criminal conduct involve a particularly high level of sophistication and complexity. These offenses are difficult to detect and require costly investigations and prosecutions. Consequently, a minimum level of 12 is provided for these offenses. Table 16–1 describes Level 6 for an offense involving computer fraud.

Application Notes

"More than minimal planning," subsection (b)(2)(A), means more planning than is typical for commission of the offense in simple form. It also exists if significant affirmative steps were taken to conceal the offense. "More than minimal planning" is deemed present in any case involving repeated acts over a period of time, unless it is clear that each instance was purely opportune.

"Scheme to defraud more than one victim," subsection (b)(2) (B), refers to a design or plan to obtain something of value from more than one person. In this context, *victim* refers to the person or entity from which the funds are to come directly.

The base offense level for 18 U.S.C., Section 1030(a)(1), "knowingly accesses a computer . . . and . . . obtains information . . . ," is set at Level 35 if the information is top secret and at Level 30 for all other national defense information. *Top secret information* is defined as information that, if disclosed, "reasonably could be expected to cause exceptionally grave damage to the national security" (from Executive Order 12356). In the case of an offense involving false

---

Table 16–1   Offenses Involving Computer-Related Fraud

(a) Base Offense Level: 6
(b) Specific Offense Characteristics
  (1) If the loss exceeded $2,000, increase the offense level as follows:

Loss (Apply the greatest)	Increase in Level
A. $2,000 or less	no increase
B. more than $2,000	add 1
C. more than $5,000	add 2
D. more than $10,000	add 3
E. more than $20,000	add 4
F. more than $40,000	add 5
G. more than $70,000	add 6
H. more than $120,000	add 7
I. more than $200,000	add 8
J. more than $350,000	add 9
K. more than $500,000	add 10
L. more than $800,000	add 11
M. more than $1,500,000	add 12
N. more than $2,500,000	add 13
O. more than $5,000,000	add 14
P. more than $10,000,000	add 15
Q. more than $20,000,000	add 16
R. more than $40,000,000	add 17
S. more than $80,000,000	add 18

  (2) If the offense involved (a) more than minimal planning, or (b) a
      scheme to defraud more than one victim, increase by two levels.
  (3) If the offense involved (a) a misrepresentation that the defendant was
      acting on behalf of a charitable, educational, religious or political orga-
      nization, or a government agency, or (b) violation of any judicial or
      administrative order, injunction, decree, or process not addressed else-
      where in the guidelines, increase by two levels. If the resulting offense
      level is less than Level 10, increase to Level 10.
  (4) If the offense involved the conscious or reckless risk of serious bodily
      injury, increase by two levels. If the resulting offense level is less than
      Level 13, increase to Level 13.
  (5) If the offense involved the use of foreign bank accounts or transactions to
      conceal the true nature or extent of the fraudulent conduct, and the of-
      fense level as determined above is less than Level 12, increase to Level 12.
  (6) If the offense (a) substantially jeopardized the safety and soundness
      of a financial institution; or (b) affected a financial institution and the
      defendant derived more than $1,000,000 in gross receipts from the
      offense, increase by four levels. If the resulting offense level is less than
      Level 24, increase to Level 24.

Source: From the U.S. Sentencing Commission, *Guidelines Manual,* 1994.

identification documents or access devices, an upward departure may be warranted where the actual loss does not adequately reflect the seriousness of the conduct.

An offense shall be deemed to have "substantially jeopardized the safety and soundness of a financial institution," subsection (b)(6)(A), if, as a consequence of the offense, the institution became insolvent; substantially reduces benefits to pensioners or insureds; was unable on demand to refund fully any deposit, payment, or investment; was so depleted of its assets as to be forced to merge with another institution in order to continue active operations; or was placed in substantial jeopardy of any of the preceding.

"Gross receipts from the offense," subsection (b)(6)(B), includes all property, real or personal, tangible or intangible, that is obtained directly or indirectly as a result of such offense.

Criteria for Upward or Downward Adjustments and Departures

Adjustments to the offense level are based on the role the defendant played in committing the offense. The determination of a defendant's role is to be made on the basis of all conduct within the scope of relevant conduct section of the guidelines. Several categories applicable to computer crime are given here:

> *Abuse of Trust or Use of Special Skill*—If the defendant abused a position of public or private trust, or used a special skill, in a manner that significantly facilitated the commission or concealment of the offense, increase by two levels. Public or private trust refers to a position of trust characterized by professional or managerial discretion.
>
> *Special skill* refers to a skill not possessed by members of the general public and usually requiring substantial education, training, or licensing. In *U.S. v. Lavin*, the federal appellate court in New York City upheld a district court's imposition of a special skills sentencing enhancement where the defendant had installed electronic equipment in ATMs to obtain PINs and account numbers of bank customers. The court said the defendant used skills that were not possessed by the general public and that these skills greatly facilitated his crime.
>
> *Obstruction of Justice*—If a defendant willfully obstructs or attempts to obstruct at any stage of the administration of justice, the

offense level is increased by two levels. Obstruction of justice can include a range of actions from making false statements, threatening witnesses, to destruction of evidence.

Groups of Closely Related Counts—All counts involving substantially the same harm are grouped together into a single group. This would cover counts involving the same victim, act, transaction, or conduct. Computer-related fraud comes under this subsection.

Criminal History—A record of a defendant's past criminal conduct, such as number and type of convictions, recidivism, and patterns of career criminal behavior are evaluated and given points to determine the criminal history category in the Sentencing Table (Figure 16–1).

Acceptance of Responsibility—If the defendant clearly demonstrates acceptance of responsibility for his or her offense, decrease the offense level by two levels.

Substantial Assistance to Authorities—On motion of the government stating that the defendant has provided substantial assistance in the investigation or prosecution of another person who has committed an offense, the court may depart from the guidelines. "Substantial weight should be given to the government's evaluation of the extent of the defendant's assistance" means essentially that the prosecutor has a big weapon in determining the fate of the defendant.

DETERMINING THE SENTENCE

The defendant's sentence is based on the combined offense level, which is subject to adjustments from the categories discussed here, and from the total points that determine the criminal history category in the sentencing table. A defendant's record is relevant to sentencing because "a defendant with a record of prior criminal behavior is more culpable than a first offender and thus deserving of greater punishment."

Section 4A1.1 of the guidelines gives items and corresponding points that determine the criminal history category in the Sentencing Table (Figure 16–1). Points are tallied for: each prior sentence of imprisonment; whether the defendant committed a crime while under any criminal justice sentence; committed a crime within two years after release from prison; or was convicted for a crime of violence. Section 4A1.3 covers departures based on how well the criminal history cate-

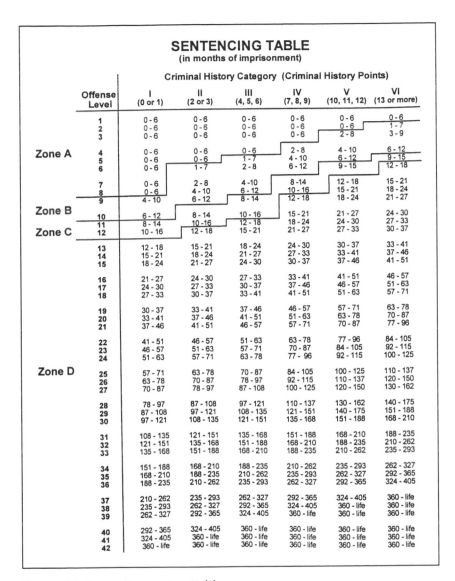

SENTENCING TABLE
(in months of imprisonment)

Criminal History Category (Criminal History Points)

		I (0 or 1)	II (2 or 3)	III (4, 5, 6)	IV (7, 8, 9)	V (10, 11, 12)	VI (13 or more)
	Offense Level						
Zone A	1	0 - 6	0 - 6	0 - 6	0 - 6	0 - 6	0 - 6
	2	0 - 6	0 - 6	0 - 6	0 - 6	0 - 6	1 - 7
	3	0 - 6	0 - 6	0 - 6	0 - 6	2 - 8	3 - 9
	4	0 - 6	0 - 6	0 - 6	2 - 8	4 - 10	6 - 12
	5	0 - 6	0 - 6	1 - 7	4 - 10	6 - 12	9 - 15
	6	0 - 6	1 - 7	2 - 8	6 - 12	9 - 15	12 - 18
	7	0 - 6	2 - 8	4 -10	8 -14	12 - 18	15 - 21
	8	0 - 6	4 - 10	6 - 12	10 - 16	15 - 21	18 - 24
Zone B	9	4 - 10	6 - 12	8 - 14	12 - 18	18 - 24	21 - 27
	10	6 - 12	8 - 14	10 - 16	15 - 21	21 - 27	24 - 30
Zone C	11	8 - 14	10 -16	12 - 18	18 - 24	24 - 30	27 - 33
	12	10 - 16	12 - 18	15 - 21	21 - 27	27 - 33	30 - 37
	13	12 - 18	15 - 21	18 - 24	24 - 30	30 - 37	33 - 41
	14	15 - 21	18 - 24	21 - 27	27 - 33	33 - 41	37 - 46
	15	18 - 24	21 - 27	24 - 30	30 - 37	37 - 46	41 - 51
	16	21 - 27	24 - 30	27 - 33	33 - 41	41 - 51	46 - 57
	17	24 - 30	27 - 33	30 - 37	37 - 46	46 - 57	51 - 63
	18	27 - 33	30 - 37	33 - 41	41 - 51	51 - 63	57 - 71
	19	30 - 37	33 - 41	37 - 46	46 - 57	57 - 71	63 - 78
	20	33 - 41	37 - 46	41 - 51	51 - 63	63 - 78	70 - 87
	21	37 - 46	41 - 51	46 - 57	57 - 71	70 - 87	77 - 96
	22	41 - 51	46 - 57	51 - 63	63 - 78	77 - 96	84 - 105
	23	46 - 57	51 - 63	57 - 71	70 - 87	84 - 105	92 - 115
	24	51 - 63	57 - 71	63 - 78	77 - 96	92 - 115	100 - 125
Zone D	25	57 - 71	63 - 78	70 - 87	84 - 105	100 - 125	110 - 137
	26	63 - 78	70 - 87	78 - 97	92 - 115	110 - 137	120 - 150
	27	70 - 87	78 - 97	87 - 108	100 - 125	120 - 150	130 - 162
	28	78 - 97	87 - 108	97 - 121	110 - 137	130 - 162	140 - 175
	29	87 - 108	97 - 121	108 - 135	121 - 151	140 - 175	151 - 188
	30	97 - 121	108 - 135	121 - 151	135 - 168	151 - 188	168 - 210
	31	108 - 135	121 - 151	135 - 168	151 - 188	168 - 210	188 - 235
	32	121 - 151	135 - 168	151 - 188	168 - 210	188 - 235	210 - 262
	33	135 - 168	151 - 188	168 - 210	188 - 235	210 - 262	235 - 293
	34	151 - 188	168 - 210	188 - 235	210 - 262	235 - 293	262 - 327
	35	168 - 210	188 - 235	210 - 262	235 - 293	262 - 327	292 - 365
	36	188 - 235	210 - 262	235 - 293	262 - 327	292 - 365	324 - 405
	37	210 - 262	235 - 293	262 - 327	292 - 365	324 - 405	360 - life
	38	235 - 293	262 - 327	292 - 365	324 - 405	360 - life	360 - life
	39	262 - 327	292 - 365	324 - 405	360 - life	360 - life	360 - life
	40	292 - 365	324 - 405	360 - life	360 - life	360 - life	360 - life
	41	324 - 405	360 - life	360 - life	360 - life	360 - life	360 - life
	42	360 - life	360 - life	360 - life	360 - life	360 - life	360 - life

Figure 16–1   Sentencing Table

gory reflects the seriousness of the defendant's past criminal conduct or the likelihood that the defendant will commit other crimes.

On the table, the Offense Level forms the vertical axis; the Criminal History (I–VI), the horizontal axis. The intersection of the Offense Level and Criminal History Category displays the guideline range in months of imprisonment.

preventing and detecting criminal conduct." That a program may fail to detect a specific offense does not mean the program is ineffective, according to the commission: "The hallmark of an effective program to prevent and detect violations of law is that the organization exercised due diligence in seeking to prevent and detect criminal conduct by its employees and other agents."

The commission describes *organizational due diligence* as including at least the following steps:

1. The organization must have established compliance standards and procedures to be followed by its employees and other agents that are reasonably capable of reducing the prospect of criminal conduct.
2. Specific individual(s) within high-level personnel of the organization must have been assigned overall responsibility to oversee compliance with such standards and procedures.
3. The organization must have used due care not to delegate substantial discretionary authority to individuals whom the organization knew, or should have known through the exercise of due diligence, had a propensity to engage in illegal activities.
4. The organization must have taken steps to communicate effectively its standards and procedures to all employees and other agents (e.g., by requiring participation in training programs or by disseminating publications that explain in a practical manner what is required).
5. The organization must have taken reasonable steps to achieve compliance with its standards (e.g., by utilizing monitoring and auditing systems reasonably designed to detect criminal conduct by its employees and other agents and by having in place and publicizing a reporting system whereby employees and other agents could report criminal conduct by others within the organization without fear of retribution).
6. The standards must have been consistently enforced through appropriate disciplinary mechanisms, including, as appropriate, discipline of individuals responsible for the failure to detect an offense. Adequate discipline of individuals responsible for an offense is a necessary component of enforcement; however, the form of discipline that will be appropriate will be case-specific.
7. After an offense has been detected, the organization must have taken all reasonable steps to respond appropriately to the offense and to prevent further similar offenses, including any

necessary modifications to its program to prevent and detect violations of law.

COMPANY-SPECIFIC COMPLIANCE PROGRAMS

Compliance programs cannot be uniform; each company must develop its own, and it should be designed to be effective in preventing and detecting violations of law within the organization.* Several factors can be used to develop a program:

1. *Size of the organization*—How formal and elaborate a compliance program will depend on the size and complexity of the organization. A larger organization should have written policies describing prohibitions to specific acts and procedures to be followed by employees and agents.
2. *The likelihood that certain offenses may occur because of the nature of the organization's business*—Where there is substantial risk that certain types of violations may occur, management must have taken steps to prevent and detect those types of offenses.
3. *Prior history of the organization*—This should indicate the types of offenses the organization should have taken steps to prevent. "Recurrence of misconduct similar to that which an organization has previously committed casts doubt on whether it took all reasonable steps to prevent such misconduct."

Lowering Culpability Scores

If an offense occurs despite an effective compliance program, three points are subtracted. This does not apply

> If an individual within high-level personnel of the organization, a person within high-level personnel of the unit of the organization within which the offense was committed where the unit had 200 or more employees, or an individual responsible for the administration or enforcement of a program to prevent and detect violations of law

---

Note: "An organization's failure to incorporate and follow applicable industry practice or the standards called for by any applicable governmental regulation weighs against a finding of an effective program to prevent and detect violations of law" (U.S. Sentencing Commission, 1994).

provide financial incentives and several important legal benefits, the question for corporations is: Do compliance programs have traps that offset potential rewards? To try to answer that question definitively is impossible because the guidelines will certainly be subject to much judicial interpretation and review. We can, however, examine some pros and cons of compliance, ideas that should be considered in establishing a company-specific program.

SETTING UP AN EFFECTIVE COMPLIANCE PROGRAM

Organizational Due Diligence

The Sentencing Commission guidelines call for the establishment of an effective program to prevent and detect violations of law. Having an effective program means that the organization has exercised due diligence. There must, however, be a number of concrete and workable actions taken by the organization to demonstrate due diligence. In other words, a paper plan is insufficient, as is a program embodied in a manual; a proactive, operating program is required. The following steps should be considered the minimum for an effective compliance program and used as an outline guide.

Ethics and Codes of Conduct

The guidelines call for the organization to establish "compliance standards and procedures . . . reasonably capable of reducing the prospect of criminal conduct." This means written ethics policies and codes of conduct that discourage and deter unethical and illegal behavior. The codes should be distributed to management and employees and contain specific prohibitions. It has been shown that written codes of conduct, adopted and adhered to by top management, can have a positive effect in deterring unlawful behavior in the organization. According to Bologna (1991):

> Research indicates that controlling unethical conduct in organizations is largely a matter of role modeling. If one's superiors and peers behave ethically, one tends to conform to the standard. Second, after role modeling, the next best defense is the establishment of a corporate code of ethics and an anti-crime or theft policy.

Thirdly, the establishment of the code isn't the end of the problem. The code must be enforced. Enforcement procedures should also be spelled out so that violations get reported, investigated and disposed of.

Assigning Oversight

The compliance program must have specific individual(s) in charge within the organization's high-level personnel. In addition, the organization must have used due care not to delegate substantial discretionary authority to persons the organization knew or should have known had a propensity to engage in illegal activities.

Several arguments have been advanced over who should be in charge of compliance programs. Legal counsel is a good candidate because compliance programs rely on employees knowing which laws and regulations are critical and specific to the organization as well as general legal prohibitions. Another candidate for compliance officer is the manager of internal auditing because a knowledge of internal controls and auditing is essential to an effective compliance program.

But experience has shown it is the tone at the top of an organization that is the key to effective compliance. Responsibility for the integrity of an organization begins and ends with the chief executive. Only top management's attitude and support can create and maintain an effective overall control environment. And, it has been argued that dishonesty is often a by-product of mismanagement. Therefore, the person or persons in charge of the compliance program should be either the top officer or drawn from top management. The guidelines, in calling for someone of high ethical stature, may mean that organizations will have to create and document effective screening measures.

Communicating Compliance Requirements

The guidelines require that there be effective communication of organizational ethics policies and codes of conduct to all employees and agents. This may be done by requiring participation in training programs or by disseminating publications to explain what is required in a practical manner. There is no commentary in the guidelines that expands on this, leaving it to the organization to come up dangers of prosecution and conviction for illegal acts. Any program needs to incorporate an awareness that it can offer possible benefits, including limits on corporate liability and awards for punitive damages, reduction of criminal penalties, and the positive public relations of being viewed as a good corporate citizen. The sentencing guidelines offer organizations flexibility in setting up a compliance program. This allows an organization to identify the acts it must prevent so that it can focus its educational activities in those areas.

A compliance program must be a serious effort. Ethics policies and codes of conduct should be adopted by the board of directors or by a committee of the board. The code should be reviewed and updated periodically. High-level officers responsible for program oversight should make periodic reports to the board or committee.

Remember the one strike and you're out rule: If a high-level individual responsible for the compliance program is involved in, condones, or is willfully ignorant of an offense, this results in a "rebuttable presumption"—that the organization did not have an effective compliance program.

Finally, the compliance program must be active and ongoing; it cannot be static. Policies, codes, controls, audits, investigations, enforcement, and responses must be monitored, reviewed, and updated in light of new legal developments and organizational experiences. Retraining will be necessary for the same reasons. In addition, the results of audits and investigations must be acted on.

18

Internal Controls and Safeguards to Prevent and Detect Fraud

Organizations face new responsibilities for protecting assets and for reporting on the effectiveness of internal controls. In addition, it is critical that the relationship between internal controls and compliance programs be fully understood. As described in Chapter 17 on compliance programs, internal controls are required, but no concrete definition was put forth by the U.S. Sentencing Commission guidelines. We shall attempt to remedy that situation by giving a brief history and analysis of the currently accepted definitions of internal controls.

Mandated internal loss-prevention controls have moved closer to reality now that the General Accounting Office (GAO) and the Committee of Sponsoring Organizations (COSO) of the Treadway Commission have settled their differences over how broad the scope of internal controls should be; specifically, whether internal controls should cover just financial reporting or extend to controls related to safeguarding assets, which normally fall under operational controls.

a report stating management's responsibilities for preparing financial statements, and for establishing a yearly assessment of "the effectiveness of such internal control structures and procedures."

ACCOUNTING PROFESSION COMPLIANCE AUDITS STANDARD

The American Institute of Certified Public Accountants (AICPA) has issued rules on the accountant's role in examining management's assertion about the effectiveness of an entity's internal control structure and whether such assertion is similar to that made by outside examining auditors. A standard, Compliance Attestation, covers internal compliance controls that follow COSO in presenting a criteria for internal control system effectiveness.

Independent accountants and auditors are being engaged to perform audits on an organization's compliance with various laws, regulations, grants, and so on. These audits are requested by the organization, but they can help satisfy a regulatory agency and others that the organization is in compliance. Outside auditors may be called on to review the current compliance efforts and suggest ways the organization can beef up its internal controls over compliance.

The AICPA's Auditing Standards Board has issued the Statement on Standards for Attestation Engagements (SSAE), No. 3—Compliance Attestation. This standard is for independent accountants hired by the management of an entity to: evaluate management's written assertion about their entity's compliance with laws, regulations, rules, or grants; assess the effectiveness of the entity's internal control structure over compliance; or both of these.

The purpose of the compliance audit is to assist users—regulators, the board of directors, contract officers—in evaluating management's assertions. The users also decide the procedures to be performed in the audit; these are called agreed-on procedures. For evaluating the effectiveness of an entity's internal control structure for compliance, management can use the COSO criteria and general framework (see previous discussion of COSO in this chapter). However, for some compliance areas more detailed and specialized criteria may be needed, such as that from a regulatory agency.

SSAE No. 3 repeated that the emphasis is on management's responsibility for:

a) identifying applicable compliance requirements
b) establishing and maintaining internal control structure policies and procedures to provide reasonable assurance that the entity complies with those requirements
c) evaluating and monitoring the entity's compliance
d) specifying reports that satisfy legal, regulatory, or contractual requirements.

The independent auditor's report should simply be in the form of procedures and findings; it "should not provide negative assurance about whether management's assertion is fairly stated." Management's assertion should be capable of evaluation against reasonable criteria already established. This can also be backed up with sufficient evidential material gathered from the entity. Findings of noncompliance during the audit are evaluated for materiality and for disclosure by management to the appropriate regulatory body.

THE GAO AND COSO REACH A CONSENSUS

As mentioned earlier, the GAO had several objections to the COSO report. In October 1992, the GAO charged that the COSO report "does not advocate public reporting on internal controls for financial reporting and fails to encourage evaluation of other controls. . . ." Also, the report "excludes safeguarding of assets from financial reporting controls, which is actually a step backward from those controls long associated with financial reporting . . . "; and "the reporting suggested by COSO would be more limited than the scope of the system of controls addressed by the Foreign Corrupt Practices Act."

After several months of discussion, COSO published an addendum to the report, and in May 1994, U.S. Comptroller General Charles Bowsher wrote COSO stating:

> The addendum provides a good working definition of safeguarding controls and criteria for judging their effectiveness. We support the COSO position that it is important for management reports to external parties on controls over financial reporting to also cover controls over safeguarding of assets. . . . With the addendum, we believe the COSO Framework merits general acceptance for evaluating the effectiveness of internal controls.

(5) Recorded recollection—a memorandum or recording that will reflect the knowledge or memory of the witness;

(6) Records of regularly conducted activity—business records, memos, reports or data compilations, in any form, of "acts, events, conditions, opinions, or diagnoses . . . or of information transmitted. . ."

(7) Absence of entry in records kept in accordance with the provisions of paragraph (6); evidence that a record normally kept is missing.

Rule 1006 covers summaries, which are: "the contents of voluminous writings, recordings, or photographs which cannot conveniently be examined in court may be presented in the form of a chart, summary or calculation." Again, originals or duplicates must be made available to other parties in the litigation at a reasonable time and place.

Subpoenas

A subpoena may require the person to appear in court to give sworn testimony at a certain time, date, and place. (A letter like the one in Appendix 19–1 usually precedes an actual subpoena.) A subpeona *duces tecum* is a subpoena that also requires the possible production of records in the possession of or under the control of an individual or an organization's "custodian" (see Appendices 19–2 through 19–7). Appendix 19–8 is a sample script for a grand jury hearing.

Search Warrants

Under the Federal Rules of Criminal Procedure, Rule 41(b), a warrant may be issued to search for and seize any "property that constitutes evidence of the commission of a criminal offense; or . . . property designed or intended for use which is or has been used as a means of committing a criminal offense."

To be issued, a search warrant must identify the property to be searched and the documents or records to be seized (i.e., the warrant must satisfy the Fourth Amendment's particularity requirement). If records are in a computer, the computer may be placed under constructive seizure until the government can understand the operating sytem and then run the computer's programs and generate all the documents and records specified in the search warrant.

In some instances, the government may choose to use a search warrant to ensure that documents are not altered or destroyed, and seizure under a search warrant obviates any Fifth Amendment claims. Finally, search warrants allow the entering of premises to serve and execute the warrant; this can also provide the opportunity to talk to employees, thus gathering information that is not privileged.

Duty-to-Report Laws

A number of federal and state laws and regulations require disclosure of corporate activities that are either illegal or arguably illegal. For instance, federal securities law requires the disclosure of any information that is economically material; in other words, it must affect a reasonable investor's investment decision. Among the banking laws are sections on money laundering and the obligation to disclose "suspected illegal activity" on the part of a customer. Reporting and disclosure laws often have gray areas in definitions of proscribed behavior plus requirements to disclose more than just completed formal reports—the "working papers" in all forms, hardcopy and electronic, are required.

Access to Corporate and Commercial Enterprise Records

Although bank and telephone records provide significant evidence to prosecutors, the most significant source of evidence lies within the realm of the books and records of commercial enterprises. For example, records from credit card companies reveal how and where a suspect spends money; and because card-issuing companies keep monthly accounts for several years, investigators can reconstruct the pattern of the suspect's expenditures over a significant period of time. Similarly, car rental agencies, airlines, hotels, and credit reporting bureaus can provide valuable material.

Law enforcement officials can often obtain commercial records on oral request alone. Under current law, privacy interests are defined can be invoked by a corporation as well as individuals; (2) only communications that are for legal purposes are protected; (3) the holder of the privilege is the client; (4) within limitations, the privilege covers communications between the corporation and in-house counsel; and (5) the privilege may be lost if a privileged document is disclosed or information shared with a third party.

The Work-Product Doctrine   This privilege is embodied in the Federal Rules of Civil Procedure, Rule 26(b)(3). Even though a party is seeking discovery and making the required showing, "the court shall protect against disclosure of mental impressions, conclusions, opinions, or legal theories of an attorney or other representative of a party concerning the litigation."

Two things to note: (1) this is a federal standard, and (2) the doctrine protects both the attorney and the client. The work-product doctrine is normally used to protect documents and information prepared in anticipation of litigation such as an internal corporate investigation. The protection has been upheld, provided the investigation is under the supervision of legal counsel.

Work-product protection can be waived and can be overcome, most assuredly, if legal counsel's representation of the client is in furtherance of a crime. In *Upjohn Co. v. United States* (1980), the government sought, through an IRS summons, corporate attorney memoranda of interviews of employees relating to foreign corrupt practices. Although it declined to "lay down a broad rule or series of rules to govern all conceivable future questions" concerning the attorney-client privilege in the corporate context, the Supreme Court nonetheless took a significant step in broadening the privilege.

The Court rejected the control-group test because it protected only communications between a lawyer and those corporate officers and agents who direct the corporation's response to the lawyer's advice. The problem with this, Justice Rehnquist wrote for the majority, was that it overlooked the fact that the privilege protects not only the lawyer's giving of advice, but also the client's giving of information. The information the lawyer needs to formulate his advice is as likely to be possessed by middle- or lower-level employees as by top management. Justice Rehnquist also stressed the lack of certainty about how "control group" should be defined. This uncertainty made it difficult for corporate attorneys and officers and employees to know whether particular conversations will be protected. The result is "to limit the valuable efforts of corporate counsel to ensure their client's compliance with the law" (*Upjohn* 101 S.Ct. at 684).

With respect to the specific facts before the Court in *Upjohn*, Justice Rehnquist concluded that the communications were clearly privileged. Upjohn's employees were ordered by their supervisors to respond to questionnaires from in-house counsel, who was to use the information provided solely to formulate legal advice concerning the company's possible involvement in illegal pay-offs. The legal implication of the investigation was made clear to the employees, the matters were within the scope of their duties, and they were told to consider their answers highly confidential.

In *Hickman v. Taylor*, the Supreme Court held that the work-product doctrine protects materials prepared "in the course of preparation for possible litigation." The term "possible litigation" is sufficiently flexible so that the work-product doctrine extends to material prepared or collected before litigation actually commences. On the other hand, some possibility of litigation must exist. Courts and commentators have offered a variety of formulas for the necessary nexus between the creation of the material and the prospect of litigation. Several commentators have suggested that:

> Prudent parties anticipate litigation, and begin preparation prior to the time suit is formally commenced. Thus the test should be whether, in light of the nature of the document and the factual situation in the particular case, the document can fairly be said to have been prepared or obtained because of the prospect of litigation.

Thus, in the context of in-house investigations, most corporate and retained attorneys will have to argue that their investigation concerned suspected criminal violations and that further investigation confirmed that suspicion, making litigation of some sort almost inevitable. The most obvious possibilities include criminal prosecutions, derivative suits, and securities litigation. Moreover, the potential for litigation is often intensified by a corporation's legal obligations to report any wrongdoing to its stockholders and to various governmental agencies.

are purged in the context of a notice of pending litigation, spoliation charges and penalties could follow.

Organizations face a dilemma: How to control potentially damaging evidence from getting into the hands of the plaintiff or prosecution and, at the same time, avoid court-imposed sanctions for destroying discoverable evidence. This dilemma is the crux of any information/evidence policy.

Conclusion

In brief, organizations should establish a document retention and destruction policy that is bonafide, consistent and reasonable; communicated to end users; descriptive on how, when, and what to purge; monitored and provided with oversight; and provable—be sure there is credible evidence that the policy was put into practice.

APPENDIX 19-1

Model Letter to a Target of an Investigation

[INSERT TARGET'S NAME AND ADDRESS]

Dear [INSERT TARGET'S NAME]:

This letter is to advise you that you are now one of the subjects of a federal grand jury investigation in this District into [INSERT BRIEF, GENERAL DESCRIPTION OF THE SUBJECT MATTER OF THE INVESTIGATION], and other matters, in possible violation of federal criminal law.

The grand jury has asked me to extend to you an invitation to appear before the grand jury at 10:00 A.M., [INSERT DAY], to testify about the matters that are now under investigation. The grand jury has also requested documents described in the attachment to this letter.* You or your authorized representative may deliver those documents to the grand jury at 10:00 A.M. on [INSERT DAY], [INSERT DATE], or if you wish, you may have those documents delivered to the office of the U.S. Attorney, as agent for the grand jury, at any earlier time that is convenient for you.

You must understand that a decision by you to testify and/or to produce the documents requested is completely voluntary and that your testimony and the documents could be used against you if any criminal charges should be returned against you.

I would appreciate it if you would ask your attorney to notify me in writing by [INSERT DAY], [INSERT DATE], as to whether or not you will accept the grand jury's invitation to testify and produce the requested documents. If your attorney has not contacted this office by that date, I will assume that you do not wish to testify.

Very truly yours,

United States Attorney

By:_____

[INSERT NAME]
Assistant U.S. Attorney

---

*Attachments should describe the documents that are sought with the same specificity otherwise employed in a subpoena *duces tecum*.

APPENDIX 19-2
Grand Jury Order

GRAND JURY ORDER DIRECTING WITNESS TO FURNISH
RECORDS, DOCUMENTS, AND PAPERS

UNITED STATES DISTRICT COURT

_____ DISTRICT OF_____

_____ DIVISION

IN RE   :   MISCELLANEOUS NO.:_____

WITNESS BEFORE THE GRAND JURY: O R D E R

On petition of the United States Attorney
for the _____ District of _____,
the Court having considered said petition
finds:

1. The Grand Jury for the _____ District of _____, _____ Division, is now
conducting an investigation involving possible

violations of _____

_____.

2. The witness, _____ , has been
duly subpoenaed *duces tecum* and has appeared
before the Grand Jury of this District Court

on _____, 19___. On that occasion, the
foreman of the Grand Jury directed the witness
to produce the records, documents, and papers
the witness was directed to furnish, as more
fully set forth in the petition of the United
States Attorney. On that occasion, the witness
refused to furnish said records, documents,

and papers asserting _____ constitutional

privilege. Said privilege was improperly asserted by the witness. The witness has no constitutional privilege to refuse to furnish the records, documents, and papers demanded by the Grand Jury.

IT IS, THEREFORE, ORDERED that _____

_____ furnish forthwith before and to the Grand Jury of the United States District

Court for the _____ District of _____, the records, documents, and papers, to wit:

_____

_____

_____.

So Ordered,

_____
United States District Judge

United States Attorney

_____
Assistant U.S. Attorney

APPENDIX 19–3

Letter to Custodian of Bank Records

Custodian of Records
[INSERT NAME AND ADDRESS OF BANK]

Re: <u>Grand Jury Subpoena Duces Tecum</u>

Dear Sir or Madam:

You are being served with a subpoena for records which requires that certain records be delivered to the United States Grand Jury for

the District of _____. Please contact Assistant U.S. Attorney [INSERT NAME] on receipt of this subpoena.

You have the right to present the records, whose production is commanded by the subpoena, directly to the Grand Jury. However, in lieu of personally appearing before the Grand Jury, you may, if you wish, comply with the subpoena by turning over the records described to any duly authorized agent of the Grand Jury or to me, prior to the date of your appearance.

You will also find enclosed a form on which you may request reimbursement by the Department of Justice of authorized expenses incurred by you in producing records under the terms of the subpoena. You <u>must</u> complete and sign the form in order to obtain any reimbursement. Requests for reimbursement <u>will</u> <u>not</u> be honored if the Department of Justice reimbursement form is not returned as requested. Finally, you will find enclosed a notice containing information about the expenses for which you may be authorized to obtain reimbursement under the terms of the Right to Financial Privacy Act of 1978.

Very truly yours,
United States Attorney

By: _____

[INSERT NAME]
Assistant U.S. Attorney

APPENDIX 19–4

Sample Corporate Records Subpoena Attachment

Any and all originals of the following documents (and copies thereof made before service of this subpoena), in your custody or subject to your control, for the period [INSERT TIME PERIOD DESIRED]:

1. All corporate ledgers and journals of the [INSERT NAME OF CORPORATION] (hereinafter referred to as the "corporation"), including the general ledger, cash receipts journal, sales journal, cash disbursements journal, voucher register, and any other ledgers and journals maintained by the corporation.
2. All banking records of the corporation, including (a) bank statements, canceled checks, checkbooks, check stubs or registers, check vouchers, and deposit clips; (b) all savings account records; (c) all records of certificates of deposit and other time deposits purchased or redeemed; and (d) records of all safe deposit boxes.
3. All records of loans received and made by the corporation, including any and all correspondence related to such loans.
4. All corporate minutes and/or other records or recordings, of any kind whatsoever, of corporate meetings and the corporate charter and by-laws, including any revisions and amendments thereto.
5. All financial statements prepared by or on behalf of the corporation.
6. All retained copies of federal, state, and local tax returns for the years [INSERT YEARS DESIRED], and working papers used in the preparation of such returns.
7. Corporate stock ledgers.
8. All vendor invoices and statements of accounts, customer billing invoices and statements of account, vouchers, and other records used in determining gross income

continued

deductions, and the balance sheet reflected on the corporate income tax returns.

9. All records in any way connected with the acquisition or sale of real and/or leasehold property by the corporation, either improved or unimproved, including purchase contracts, settlement sheets, contracts of sale, deeds, notes, mortgages, deeds of trust, leases, correspondence, memoranda, and notes of meetings and/or telephone calls.

10. All records of tangible and intangible personal property legally or equitably owned by the corporation, including, for example, stock and bonds.

11. All records relating to corporation construction loan agreements and mortgages, draws, fees, and permanent financing commitments and mortgages, including all correspondence, memoranda, notes, and other materials relating thereto.

12. All personnel files of current and former employees and consultants.

13. All U.S. Information Returns (Forms 1096 and 1099), Employer's Quarterly Federal Tax Returns (Form 941), and Employer's Annual Federal Unemployment Tax Returns (Form 940) filed by the corporation.

14. All travel and entertainment records.

15. All records of commissions, rebates, discounts, bonuses, gifts, or other payments made by the corporation or by any of its members, to any person or entity who is not an officer, director, manager, member, or employee.

16. All agreements, contracts, memoranda of understanding, and other such documents, reflecting or containing any agreement between the corporation, on the one hand, and any of the following individuals or entities, or any entity of which any such individual is an owner, officer, director, manager, partner, or employee, on the other hand:

[INSERT NAMES OF INDIVIDUALS AND ENTITIES]

APPENDIX 19–5
Sample Bank Subpoena Attachment

Any and all original documents (or micro-
film copies where originals are not available),
in the bank's custody or subject to its control, that in any way relate to any of the
following persons and entities, or to any
checking, savings, or loan accounts for, by,
or on behalf of them either individually or
on behalf of, in trust for, or in combination
with any other person or entity for the period
[INSERT TIME PERIOD DESIRED],

    [INSERT LIST OF NAMES OF PERSONS AND ENTITIES
        WHOSE RECORDS ARE SUBPOENAED]

including, but not limited to, the following
documents:

1. Signature cards of all accounts
2. Monthly checking statements
3. Copies of all canceled checks
4. Transcripts of savings accounts
5. Copies of deposit slips for checking and
   savings accounts, and deposit items to
   which those slips relate
6. Loan records, including collateral loan
   records
7. Loan ledger sheets
8. Safe deposit box records of access
9. Financial statements and credit reports
10. Copies of promissory notes
11. Mortgage records and applications
12. Copies of certificates of deposit
13. Investment and/or custodian accounts
14. Records of purchase or bearer bonds
15. Safekeeping register records
16. Records of transfer of funds by wire or
    collection
17. Receipts of delivery of securities
18. Copies of application for purchase of man-
    ager's checks, cashier's checks, and/or
    treasurer's checks, together with the
    checks that were purchased.

APPENDIX 19–6

Sample Accountant's Records Subpoena Attachments

Any and all original documents (and copies thereof made before service of this subpoena), in your custody or subject to your control, whether owned by you or by anyone else, that in any way relate to the following persons and entities, whether individually or in combination with any other person or entity, for the period [INSERT TIME PERIOD DESIRED],

[INSERT NAMES OF PERSONS AND ENTITIES
WHOSE RECORDS ARE SUBPOENAED]

including, but not limited to, the following materials:

- federal and state tax returns, including retained copies thereof
- working papers
- financial statements
- check spreads
- audit reports and other records of financial examinations
- correspondence, memoranda, notes, and copies of documents prepared for filing with any agency of the federal government, any state or local government, or any bank or other financial institution

APPENDIX 19–7

Sample Questions for a Records Custodian Witness

1. State your name, address, and occupation.
2. Did you (or did the managing officer of your employer) receive a subpoena to bring to this Grand Jury certain documents and records?
3. Were you directed or instructed by your employer to appear today with the records and documents described in the subpoena?
4. Have you read the subpoena?
5. Did you understand what you read?
6. Did you discuss this subpoena with an attorney? If so, identify the attorney.
7. Did you search for the records described in the subpoena?
8. How did you conduct your search for these records?
9. Did anyone assist you in this search? Who?
10. Did you locate all of the records described in the subpoena?
11. Is there any record described in the subpoena that you could not or did not find?
12. Do you now have with you each, every, and all records and documents that are to be produced before the Grand Jury? If not, why not?
13. Identify each document you have with you.
14. Does this Grand Jury now have every document and record that the subpoena directed you to produce?

After making a record of the answers to these questions, request the Foreperson to designate the Case Agent as the Agent of the Grand Jury to take possession of the documents and to retain all of the same, subject to further order of the Grand Jury.

APPENDIX 19–8

Sample Grand Jury Script

1. [WITNESS SWORN BY FOREPERSON] State and spell name for the record.

2. Are you here (pursuant to a subpoena) (voluntarily)?

3. Do you understand that everything that is said during these proceedings is being recorded by the court reporter?

4. You are appearing before a duly impanelled federal Grand Jury inquiring into possible violations of federal law, including, but not limited to, [CITE SPECIFIC SECTIONS AND VIOLATIONS UNLESS HARMFUL TO THE INVESTIGATION AND SUPPORTED BY MEMO TO FILE].

   You are appearing because it is believed you may have certain information (and/or documents) relevant to that investigation. Do you understand that?

5. You have certain rights as a witness before this Grand Jury which I am about to explain to you.

   a. First, you have the right, under the Sixth Amendment of the U.S. Constitution, to advice of counsel. That is, you may be represented by an attorney. Your attorney, if you have one, cannot be in the Grand Jury room with you but you may, at any time, advise the Foreperson that you would like to consult with your attorney. You may then leave the Grand Jury room, consult with your attorney, and return.

      Do you understand that right?
      Do you presently have an attorney?
      If yes, what is your attorney's name?
      Have you consulted with your attorney?
      Is your attorney outside?

Do you want time to arrange for your
attorney to be here?

Do you have any questiions regarding
your right to advice of counsel?

b. Second, you have the Fifth Amendment
right to refuse to answer any question
asked of you if you honestly and truly
believe the answer may tend to incriminate you. An answer may tend to incriminate you if it can provide or lead to
information regarding a crime for which
you can be prosecuted.

Do you understand that right?

Do you understand that anything you
may say can be used against you?

[ALTERNATE-A witness normally has a
privilege to refuse to answer questions
that may tend to incriminate him or her.
However, the District Court has issued
an order of immunity whereby any statement you give in these proceedings may
not be used against you nor may any
statement be used to obtain other information against you.

Do you understand that you have
immunity?

Do you understand that anything
you say cannot be used against
you?]

6. You are hereby advised that you are a "target" of this investigation. That means we
have substantial evidence linking you to a
crime and you are considered to be someone
who may be indicted.

7. Have any promises or threats been made by
the government, either directly by its
agents and attorneys or indirectly through
your attorney?

An Outline and Checklist of Legal Issues for Corporate Investigations

An internal investigation is part of the defense of the corporation against possible compliance-related liability. The purpose of the investigation is to gather information for legal advice to be given to the corporation. Specific actions taken and techniques used in an investigation will be directed at uncovering all required information that will be helpful in clarifying the corporation's litigation risk exposure and minimizing the damage that could arise from such exposure.

The following outline and checklist highlights the more significant steps to take and the questions to examine in developing a planned, efficient response to compliance litigation risk.

I. Types of misconduct that would or should trigger an internal investigation:
   A. Possible criminal misconduct by senior officers or managers
   B. Misconduct that produces possible liability for the corporation

II. Why an internal investigation should be done in the face of potentially criminal conduct:
   A. To develop firsthand knowledge of the facts exposing the organization and its officers to harm
   B. To deal with the situation before government awareness and action
   C. Help shape the prosecutor's understanding of the problem
   D. Avoid an indictment or debarment from government contracts
   E. Avoid a conviction

III. When to initiate an internal investigation:
   A. The organization becomes aware that its officers or other high-level employees have been or are involved in conduct that may expose the organization to criminal, civil, or administrative liability or sanction, or harm the organization's reputation
   B. The implications are fully understood, that is, the target is known, whether the conduct is systemic, the legal risk exposures have been identified, and possible damages estimated.

IV. Elements of the investigation plan:
   A. What is the nature and source of possible personnel misconduct, government investigation, or litigation?
      1. Rumor, accusation, gossip; list any credible sources
      2. Media story
      3. Industry as a whole said to be probable target of government hearings or investigation
      4. Company fraud or ethics hotline, audits, compliance reviews, vendor complaints
      5. Whistleblower suit said to be developing
      6. Grand jury target letter received
      7. Grand jury subpoena received
      8. Law enforcement contact, search warrant, administrative summons, or civil investigative demand from a government agency
      9. Indictment
      10. Parallel proceedings started simultaneously
   B. Type of misconduct:
      1. Criminal

    2. Civil

    3. Regulatory

C. Who is involved and is the misconduct systemic?

    1. Single, rogue employee

    2. Employees and lower-level management

    3. Mid-level management

    4. Senior officers

D. What is the level of seriouness and corporate exposure to the risk of:

    1. Criminal liability

    2. Substantial monetary damages

    3. Injury to reputation

    4. Other significant harm

E. Does a finding of misconduct require disclosure to federal or state authorities?

    1. Voluntary disclosure

    2. Disclosure is optional

F. If the disclosure is optional, what are the risks and benefits of voluntary disclosure?

G. Who should direct the internal investigation?

    1. In-house counsel

    2. Outside counsel

    3. Other

H. What resources should be used to conduct an efficient internal investigation?

    1. In-house auditors and investigators

    2. Auditors, investigators, and technicians hired and controlled by outside counsel

    3. Combination of in-house and outside auditors and investigators

I. Adopt board of directors resolution for internal investigation (see sample resolution in Appendix 20–1)

J. Information control-and-access strategies:

    1. In internal corporate investigations of possible criminal misconduct, the defense and prosecution have distinct strategies related to information.

    2. For the defense of the corporation, the strategy must be to control access to critical information—review the primary legal methods of controlling access with legal counsel: the

attorney-client privilege, the self-incrimination privilege, and the work-product rule.

3. The prosecution strategy is to gain access to as much information as possible, and usually as quickly as possible; the techniques used could include interviews, surveillance, administrative summonses, grand jury subpoenas, search warrants, and civil investigative demands.

K. Information gathering and evaluation, phase one:

1. Document reviews and identification; separate privileged documents; produce an index of documents
2. Initial audit review
3. Identify prospective interviewees—employees/agents possibly having knowledge of (1) location or removal of documents or (2) parties involved in possible wrongdoing
4. Write and distribute letter of instruction from senior executive officer or legal counsel to each employee to be interviewed: advise that the attorney represents the corporation; that employee may get personal attorney
5. Conduct survey (via interviews or form) with selected personnel
6. For all interviews, use two interviewers, counsel and legal assistant; do not produce verbatim transcripts and quotes or factual descriptions of the substance of interviews; create only summary memos and notes that contain, throughout, "counsel's mental impressions"

L. Possible criminal violation

1. It is often difficult at the outset of an investigation to establish whether there has been a specific criminal violation of a specific statute. Look for the following elements before deciding on the exact nature of the possible offense or misconduct; are there indications of:
   a. Intent to commit a wrongful act
   b. Disguise of purpose (falsities, misrepresentations)
   c. Reliance by suspect on ignorance or carelessness of victim
   d. Voluntary victim action to assist the suspect
   e. Concealment of the violation

M. Liability risk assessment

1. It should be determined if civil or criminal lawsuits or government parallel proceedings exist, are pending or contemplated in the case about to be investigated.

2. If the violation is known, review the statute(s) and assess the position of the organization regarding culpability, defenses, possible damages, cooperation with the prosecutor, voluntary disclosure, or internal resolution.

N. Case theory and evidence

Most investigations have a theory of the case at the outset. This usually means there has been a review of the applicability of particular criminal statutes to the initially known facts of the case. During information/evidence gathering, the theory of the case may be modified or develop in a different direction. This is simply a determination, based on new information, of which violations are most clearly demonstrated by the evidence gathered and what additional evidence may be required. Also determine what evidence might be needed to negate defenses.

O. Information sources

Information comes from either persons or things. In internal corporate investigations, things are usually business records and written information about specific activities of personnel and executives. Information can also come from persons inside and outside the business. To gather information most efficiently and thoroughly, it is vital for the investigator to know the system of the organization—its paper flow, disposition of documents, its procedures for claims, payments, etc. And, personnel and job functions—who is most likely to have what information.

P. Information and evidence gathering

During the course of any investigation a lot of information is gathered. Only a small portion of the total will wind up as evidence. Evidence, then, is actually distilled information. The distillation process is one of gathering, examination, and appraisal, plus a constant testing against both the theory of the case and possible violations of law.

1. Determine if the organization has done previous compliance reviews, audits, or investigations that could be useful to the current investigation.
2. If yes, determine the results to date and obtain and secure all reports and evidence gathered.
3. Determine who should be interviewed.
4. Determine which reports and documents should be examined.

Q. Review, with legal counsel, laws affecting internal investigations:
   1. Discovery privileges
   2. Document retention and destruction
   3. Employee-related law such as privacy, defamation, false imprisonment, harrassment, witness tampering, and obstruction of justice
   4. Searches and seizures
R. Issue notice to cease destruction of documents
   1. Immediately on notification from legal counsel of receipt of discovery order, complaint filed, indictment issued, or start of legal investigation.
   2. To avoid charges of obstruction of justice and court-imposed sanctions.
S. Expert witness/technical assistance
   Contact expert witnesses who may be needed for the investigation such as information systems (IS) technicians, accountants/auditors, specialists in specific areas of compliance, and so on.
T. Security and storage of evidence
   1. Mark documents, reports, surveys, interviews, and other materials relevant to the case according to its assigned level of proprietary information security
   2. Secure the documentation for possible litigation and, if necessary, lock up magnetic media, printouts, and so on, in appropriate storage such as media or fire-resistant safes
U. Case report by chief investigator
   Utilizing the evidence and testimony gathered, report the findings to legal counsel for disposition.
V. Counsel's report of findings of fact and legal opinion
   Report may be given verbally or in writing to the board of directors, the audit committee, the CEO, or other responsible corporate officers, and should cover:
   1. Case chronology
   2. Type of misconduct and degree of seriousness
   3. Individual employee(s) involved; profile possible indictable suspects(s)
   4. If misconduct systemic, give level of management and location within corporation

5. Extent of possible corporate liability; does misconduct materiality affect issues, accuracy of tax filings, fiduciary responsibilities; cite specific statute(s) for possible litigation by the government
6. Disclosure requirements; if optional disclosure, what the legal benefits and risks are
7. Give status of evidence and witnesses
8. Identify internal control weaknesses and corrective actions that should be taken
9. Summary—give an opinion on what action the government is likely to take and when

APPENDIX 20–1

Internal Corporate Investigation: Directing the Investigation

The following list suggests critical initial steps in an internal corporate investigation. It starts from the premise that an internal investigation is necessary, that a decision has been made to learn the extent and seriousness of a specific corporate problem—a problem that may or may not, at some point, lead to the notification and involvement of government or criminal justice agencies.

The objective here is to provide guidance on conducting a prompt, efficient, and diligent investigation that offers maximum legal protection to the corporate entity.

- The board of directors of the corporation meets and appoints a special committee to:
  a. Direct the investigation
  b. Retain outside counsel
- An enabling resolution by the board should say that the special committee will direct a legal study and investigation and that it should retain outside legal counsel to provide the corporation, through the special committee, legal advice based on its findings.
- Outside counsel should be a firm that has not previously given legal advice to the corporation.
- Outside legal counsel is authorized to conduct the investigation and is:
  a. Given autonomy to conduct a professional investigation and inquiry;
  b. Authorized to procure such assistance as necessary, such as independent accountants and investigators;
  c. Authorized to interview any employees of the corporation who might have knowledge of the facts;
  d. Authorized to analyze any and all information gathered from sources and materials inside and outside the corporation.
- Outside counsel should meet on a regular basis with the special committee:
  a. Minutes or some record of the meetings should be made.
  b. Obvious sensitive topics need not be recorded.
  c. Some evidence of these meetings is needed, however, to establish the diligence of the special committee and counsel.

- Conducting the internal investigation:
  a. Reporting responsibility on the investigation is only to the special committee—there is no responsibility to report to corporate management.
  b. At all times, legal counsel must make decisions on assistance and investigative materials based on attorney-client privilege and the work-product rule.
  c. If company personnel are used in the investigation, they must be instructed that during the investigation their work product and findings are to be given only to the outside legal counsel.
  d. Independent accountants, auditors, investigators, and others should be engaged to assist and report exclusively to the outside legal counsel. Again, such engagements should be set up so as not to jeopardize the attorney-client privilege or the work-product rule. Services of independent experts should be procured through outside counsel and the work done under its direction.
- Results of the work should become the exclusive property of the outside law firm; all communications to be exclusively with outside counsel, and all professional services paid for by the outside counsel.
- All of the above should be included in a retainer letter or contract between the law firm and the independent service supplier.
- At the conclusion of the investigation, outside counsel advises the special committee on its findings and suggested legal action.
- The special committee reports to the corporation's board of directors on the investigation and the advice given by outside legal counsel.
- The board of directors decides on what action, if any, to take.

References

American Law Institute. *Restatement of the Law of Torts, Second*. Section 46, Comment d., 1965.

Black, Henry Campbell. *Black's Law Dictionary*. 4th ed. rev. St. Paul: West, 1968.

———. *Black's Law Dictionary*. 5th ed. St. Paul: West, 1979.

Bologna, Jack. *Computer Crime: Wave of the Future*. Madison, WI: Assets Protection, 1981.

———. *Computer Security Digest*, May 1989, May 1990, September 1990.

———. "Corporate Ethics: The Last Word or the Lost Word," *Assets Protection*, 12(1): 3–4, 1991.

———. *Detecting and Preventing Fraud in Books of Account*. Madison, WI: Assets Protection, 1991.

———. *Handbook on Corporate Fraud*. Stoneham, MA: Butterworth-Heinemann, 1993.

Bologna, Jack, and Robert J. Lindquist. *Fraud Auditing and Forensic Accounting: New Tools and Techniques*. New York: John Wiley & Sons, 1987.

Bologna, Jack, and Paul Shaw. *Fraud Awareness Manual*. Madison, WI: Assets Protection, 1992.

Bowsher, C. "The COSO Report: A New Addendum Results in GAO Endorsement." *Journal of Accountancy* (July 1994): 18.

Clinard, Marshall B., and Peter Yeager. *Corporate Crime*. New York: Free Press; London: Collier Macmillan, 1980.

Coleman, James William. *The Criminal Elite: The Sociology of White Collar Crime*. New York: St. Martin's Press, 1985.

Committee of Sponsoring Organizations of the Treadway Commission (COSO). *Internal Control—Integrated Framework*. New York: COSO of the Treadway Commission, 1992.

————. *Reporting to External Parties* (addendum). New York: Committee of Sponsoring Organizations of the Treadway Commission, 1994.

Cressey, Donald L. *Other People's Money: A Study in the Social Psychology of Embezzlement*. Glencoe, IL: Free Press, 1953.

Deal, Terrence E., and Allen A. Kennedy, *Corporate Cultures: The Rites and Rituals of Corporate Life*. Reading, MA: Addison-Wesley, 1982.

Fricano, E., ed. *Corporate Practice Series Guide to RICO*. Washington: Bureau of National Affairs, 1986.

Geis, Gilbert. *On White-Collar Crime*. Lexington, MA: Lexington Books, 1982.

Green, Gary S. *Occupational Crime*. Chicago: Nelson-Hall, 1990.

Hollinger, Richard C., and John P. Clark. "Organizational Control and Employee Theft," *Assets Protection*, 5(5): 34–40, 1980.

Jaspan, Norman, and Hillel Black. *The Thief in the White Collar*. Philadelphia: Lippincott, 1980.

Krauss, Leonard I., and Aileen MacGahan. *Computer Fraud and Countermeasures*. Englewood Cliffs, NJ: Prentice-Hall, 1979.

National Commission on Fraudulent Financial Reporting. *Report of the National Commission on Fraudulent Financial Reporting, Exposure Draft*. Washington, April 1987.

Nettler, Gwynn. *Lying, Cheating and Stealing*. Cincinnati: Anderson Publishing Co., 1982.

Perry, William. *Computer Control and Audit*. New York: Wiley, 1984.

Sawyer, Lawrence B., Albert A. Murphy, and Michael Crossley. "Management Fraud: The Insidious Specter," *Assets Protection*, 4(2): 13–20, 1979.

Sutherland, Edwin Hardin. *White-Collar Crime*. New York: Dryden Press, 1949.

U.S. Department of the Treasury, Internal Revenue Service. *Financial Investigative Techniques*. Washington, 1979.

U.S. Congress, Senate. *Amending the Racketeer Influenced and Corrupt Organizations Act*. 101st Congress, 2d sess., 1990. S. Rpt. 269.

U.S. Sentencing Commission. *Guidelines Manual*. St. Paul: West, 1994.

Selected Additional Publications on Fraud, Law, and Investigation

Akin, Richard H. *The Private Investigator's Basic Manual*. Springfield, IL: Charles C Thomas, 1976.

American Bar Association. *American Bar Association Handbook on Antitrust Grand Jury Investigations*. Chicago: ABA, 1978.

Anacapa Sciences, Inc. *Sources of Information for Criminal Investigators*. Santa Barbara: American Security Institute, 1987.

Androphy, J. *White Collar Crime*. Colorado Springs: Shepard's/McGraw-Hill, 1992.

Arkin, Stanley, and Earl Dudley. *Business Crime: Criminal Liability of the Business Community*. New York: Matthew Bender, 1981.

Arkin, Stanley, Barry Bohrer, Don Cuneo, et al. *Prevention and Prosecution of Computer and High Technology Crime*. Albany, NY: Matthew Bender, 1989.

Audit Commission, *A Study of Internal Frauds in Banks*. Chicago: Bank Administration Institute, 1972.

Bailey, F. Lee, and Henry B. Rothblatt. *Investigation and Preparation of Criminal Cases*. Rochester, NY: Lawyers Co-operative, 1970.

Barson, Kalman A. *Investigative Accounting: Techniques and Procedures for Determining the Reality Behind the Financial Statements.* New York: Van Nostrand Reinhold Company, 1986.

Bender, David. *Computer Law: Evidence and Procedure.* New York: Matthew Bender, 1978.

Bequai, August. *White-Collar Crime: A Twentieth-Century Crisis.* Lexington, MA: D. C. Heath, 1979.

Block, Dennis J., and Marvin J. Pickholz. *The Internal Corporate Investigation.* New York: Practicing Law Institute, 1980.

Blum, Richard H. *Deceivers and Deceived.* Springfield, IL: Charles C Thomas, 1972.

Brickey, Kathleen. *Corporate Criminal Liability.* Deerfield, IL: Callaghan & Co., 1989.

Briloff, Abraham J. *Unaccountable Accounting.* New York: Harper & Row, 1972.

————. *More Debits than Credits: The Burnt Investor's Guide to Financial Statements.* New York: Harper & Row, 1976.

————. *The Truth about Corporate Accounting.* New York: Harper & Row, 1981.

Bromberg, A., and L. Lowenfels. *Securities Fraud and Commodities Fraud.* Colorado Springs: Shepard's/McGraw-Hill, Inc., 1990.

Brown, L. *The Legal Audit: Corporate Internal Investigation.* New York: Clark Boardman, 1990.

Business Conference Board. *Corporate Ethics.* New York: The Conference Board, 1990.

Comer, Michael. *Corporate Fraud.* New York: McGraw-Hill, 1977.

Coughran, Edward. *Computer Abuse and Criminal Law.* San Diego: Computer Center, University of California, 1976.

Crowley, George, and Richard Manning. *Criminal Tax Fraud—Representing the Taxpayer Before Trial.* New York: Practicing Law Institute, 1976.

Edelhertz, Herbert, Ezra Stotland, Marilyn Walsh, and Milton Weinberg. *The Investigation of White-Collar Crime.* Washington: Law Enforcement Assistance Administration, 1977.

Eichenwald, K. *Serpent on the Rock.* New York: HarperBusiness, 1995.

Elliott, Robert K., and John J. Willingham. *Management Fraud: Detection and Deterrence.* New York: Petrocelli Books, 1980.

Federal Bureau of Investigation. *Introduction to Books and Records.* Quantico, VA: FBI Academy, 1975.

Forensic Services Directory. Princeton, NJ: National Forensic Center (annual), 1990–.

Frank, P., ed. *Litigation Services Handbook.* New York: John Wiley & Sons, 1990.

Fridson, M. *Financial Statement Analysis.* New York: John Wiley & Sons, 1995.

Glekel, Jeffrey, ed. *Business Crimes: A Guide for Corporate and Defense Counsel.* New York: Practicing Law Institute, 1982.

Glick, Rush G., and Robert S. Newson. *Fraud Investigation.* Springfield, IL: Charles C Thomas, 1974.

Goldblatt, M. *Preventive Law in Corporate Practice.* New York: Matthew Bender, 1991.

Grau, J. J., and B. Jacobson. *Criminal and Civil Investigation Handbook.* New York: McGraw-Hill, 1981.

Gup, B. *Bank Fraud.* Chicago: Bank Administration Institute, 1991.

Hannon, L. *Legal Side of Private Security.* Westport, CT: Greenwood Publishing Group, 1992.

Hartsfield, H. *Investigating Employee Conduct.* Deerfield, IL: Callaghan & Co., 1988.

Jaspan, Norman. *Mind Your Own Business.* Englewood Cliffs, NJ: Prentice-Hall, 1974.

Johnson, John M., and Jack Douglas, eds. *Crime at the Top.* Philadelphia: Lippincott, 1978.

Katzman, G. C. *Inside the Criminal Process.* New York: W. W. Norton, 1991.

Kell, William G., and Robert K. Mautz. *Internal Controls in U.S. Corporations.* New York: Financial Executives Institute Research Foundation, 1980.

Kellogg, I., and L. Kellogg. *Fraud, Window Dressing, and Negligence in Financial Statements.* Colorado Springs: Shepards/McGraw-Hill, 1991.

Kohn, E. J. *Fraud.* New York: Harper & Row, 1973.

Kramer, M.W. *Investigative Techniques in Complex Financial Crimes.* Washington: National Institute on Economic Crime, 1989.

Kropatkin, Philip, and Richard P. Kusserow. *Management Principles for Assets Protection: Understanding the Criminal Equation.* New York: John Wiley & Sons, 1986.

Kwitny, Jonathan. *The Fountain Pen Conspiracy.* New York: Alfred A. Knopf, 1973.

Leininger, Sheryl, ed. *Internal Theft: Investigation and Control: An Anthology.* Los Angeles: Security World Publishing, 1975.

Levi, M. *Regulating Fraud: White-Collar Crime and the Criminal Process.* New York: Tavistock Publications, 1988.

Loeffler, Robert M. Report of the Trustee of Equity Funding Corporation of America. Pasadena, CA: U.S. District Court for the Central District of California, October 31, 1974.

Mann, Kenneth. *Defending White-Collar Crime: A Portrait of Attorneys at Work.* New Haven and London: Yale University Press, 1985.

Miller, Gordon H. *Prosecutor's Manual on Computer Crimes.* Decatur, GA: Prosecuting Attorneys' Council of Georgia, 1978.

Miller, Norman C. *The Great Salad Oil Swindle.* New York: Coward McCann, 1965.

Nossen, Richard. *The Determination of Undisclosed Financial Interest.* Washington: Government Printing Office, 1979.

Obermaier, H. *White Collar Crime.* New York: Law & Seminars Press, 1990.

O'Neill, Robert. *Investigative Planning.* Report prepared for Battelle Law and Justice Study Center, Seattle, 1978.

Parker, Donn B. *Crime by Computer.* New York: Charles Scribner's Sons, 1976.

Payne, S. *Art of Asking Questions.* Princeton, NJ: Princeton University Press, 1979.

Roddy, K. *RICO in Business and Commercial Litigation.* Colorado Springs: Shepard's/McGraw-Hill, 1992.

Russell, Harold F. *Foozles and Frauds.* Altamonte Springs, FL: Institute of Internal Auditors, 1977.

Schabeck, Tim. *Computer Crime Investigation Manual.* Madison, WI: Assets Protection, 1979.

Schilit, H. *Financial Shenanigans.* New York: McGraw-Hill, 1993.

Seidler, Lee J., Frederick Andrews, and Marc J. Epstein. *The Equity Funding Papers: The Anatomy of a Fraud.* Santa Barbara: John Wiley & Sons, 1977.

Shapiro, Susan P. *Wayward Capitalists: Target of the Securities and Exchange Commission.* New Haven and London: Yale University Press, 1984.

Sigler, J., and J. Murphy. *Corporate Lawbreaking and Interactive Compliance.* Westport, CT: Greenwood Publishing Group, 1991.

Smith, T. *Accounting for Growth: Stripping the Camouflage from Company Accounts.* London: Century Business, 1992.

Soble, Ronald L., and Robert E. Dallos. *The Impossible Dream: The Equity Funding Story, the Fraud of the Century.* New York: Putnam, 1975.

Sohn, Albert. *Techniques and Procedures Utilized in the Investigation of Economic Crimes and Official Corruption.* rev. ed. Albany: New York State Commission of Investigation, 1975.

Somers, L. *Economic Crimes: Investigative Principles and Techniques.* New York: Clark Boardman, 1984.

Sterngold, J. *Burning Down the House: How Greed, Deceit, and Bitter Revenge Destroyed E.F. Hutton.* New York: Summit Books, 1990.

Stone, C. *Where the Law Ends: Social Control of Corporate Behavior.* New York: Harper & Row, 1975.

U.S. Department of the Treasury. Internal Revenue Service. *IRS Manual: Special Agent Handbook.* Washington, 1987.

Vaughan, D. *Controlling Unlawful Organizational Behavior—Social Structure and Corporate Misconduct.* Chicago: University of Chicago Press, 1983.

Villa, J. *Banking Crimes: Fraud, Money Laundering, and Embezzlement.* New York: Clark Boardman, 1988.

Wagner, Charles. *The CPA and Computer Fraud.* Lexington, MA: Lexington Books, 1979.

Wasik, M. *Crime and the Computer.* Cary, NC: Oxford University Press, 1991.

Weisburd, D., S. Wheeler, E. Waring, and N. Bode. *Crimes of the Middle Classes: White-Collar Offenders in the Federal Courts.* New Haven: Yale University Press, 1991.

Wheeler, S., K. Mann, and A. Sarat. *Sitting in Judgment: The Sentencing of White-Collar Criminals.* New Haven: Yale University Press, 1988.

Index